EmpowerEd

USING REAL CASE
EXAMPLES TO LOOK
DEEPER INTO IEP
MANAGEMENT

Jennifer Oneal Price, Esq.

Copyright © Jennifer Oneal Price, 2019

All rights reserved. No part of this book may be reproduced or photocopied in any form or by any means, electronic or mechanical, including photocopying, recording or by any information storage and retrieval systems, without prior written permission of the publisher and/or author, except that a reviewer may quote brief passages in a review.

Disclaimer:

The information contained in this book is general information and may or may not reflect current legal developments. This book is designed to provide general information in regard to the subject matter covered. It is sold with the understanding that the publisher and/or author are not engaged in rendering legal or other professional services. For legal advice about a specific set of facts, you should consult with an attorney.

The purpose of this book is to educate and inform. While every effort has been made to make this book as accurate as possible, there may be mistakes, both typographical and in content. The author/publisher shall have neither liability nor responsibility to any person or entity with respect to any loss or damage caused, or alleged to be caused, directly or indirectly, by the information contained in this book. If you do not wish to be bound by the above, you may return the book for a full refund. Every effort has been made to ensure that no copyrighted material has been used without permission. The author regrets any oversights that may have occurred and is happy to rectify them in future printings of this book.

ISBN: 978-1-7334341-0-2

Designed by Laura Boyle

For more information about Attorney Jennifer Oneal Price, go to www.jenniferpricelaw.com

Contents

1. Introduction — 5
2. Step One — 7
3. Step Two — 15
4. Step Three — 35
5. Step Four — 65
6. Exhaustion — 75
7. Bullying and Your Disabled Child — 83
8. The Endrew F. Case — 91
9. Acknowledgments — 101
10. Case Citations — 103
11. About the Author — 111

Introduction

I know the story. Your child is having issues in school and you suspect it's not because s/he is "being bad." You request an evaluation to see if s/he qualifies for an accommodation or special education services. The test takes awhile. Why does it take so long to get an evaluation? Then, you learn your child qualifies for special education services. What comes next? Then, you get your child's Individualized Education Program, a.k.a. IEP. Why isn't the school following it? You try to have meetings with the school, only to be met with obstinance. You walk in the meeting. You see a room full of people on the "school's side." Who is there for you? You feel overwhelmed and alone. I know the story because, as an attorney who represents children with disabilities, I've heard it too many times.

The ultimate purpose of this book is to empower parents (and anyone else working as an educational advocate) about how courts rule on education cases concerning children who have disabilities - intellectual, behavioral, or physical. I include specific points of reference so you can use this as a resource guide for your own situation. Statistically, most parents in a due process hearing represent themselves in these types of legal disputes. The one consistent comment I've heard is that by the time things become this contentious with the school district, they feel overwhelmed and uninformed.

By law, public schools are required to provide a free appropriate public education (FAPE). The issue is that there are extensive and complicated statutes governing children with disabilities. There are individualized education programs (IEPs) and 504 Service Agreements. Both are created for children with disabilities, but they are designed to address different areas of need. This short book sorts out your options, offers court cases as examples, and explains the steps you can take if you are not happy with the plans made for your child's education.

As an attorney now in private practice, I spend part of each day answering telephone calls on questions from parents who are frustrated over what their school is or is not doing for their children, and concerned about what should be their next steps.

I left a District Attorney's Office after seeing worst-case scenarios in juvenile court: when learning accommodations were not made, or plans were not implemented for children with disabilities. I realized that while these were similar stories told from different situations, the common thread in all of them was either IEP or 504 Service Agreement management. After some research and talking to colleagues, I decided to go into private practice to focus on representing children with disabilities. One major hurdle I quickly learned was the lack of information many parents and advocates have, including not knowing that their children even have legal rights when it comes to education. That is why I decided to write this book. It is meant to be a guide and a starting point.

While this cannot serve as legal advice, my goal is to help parents feel a little more empowered than before they read it. This guide is designed to get you past the basics by using real court case examples to show the practical side of how courts have ruled on familiar issues. In the end, the goal is to set your child up for educational success. This book is broken up into four steps that build on each other. There is a glossary at the end to help keep track of some of the terms parents may encounter in their journey, as well as full case citations.

To you and your child's success!

Step One

What Is Child Find?

Child Find is a term of art that places a legal requirement on schools to identify, locate, and evaluate your child, but this process can also start with you, the parent. (Throughout the rest of this book, I use "parent" but I'm referring to parents, guardians, and educational advocates.)

As the parent, you know your child better than anyone else. If you see your infant son or daughter struggling to hold an object, you know whether the response will be frustration (throwing it down) or curiosity (picking it up each time it falls). You know this because you've been paying attention. This parental observation remains true for noticing developmental delays. I put Child Find as the first step for parents for a few reasons. You will know whether a behavior is typical or atypical. You're with your child from the beginning, so you become a first line of defense. This places you in the best position to be proactive and address any potential developmental delays as early as possible.

Early diagnosis has been attributed to improving a child's long-term educational success. Since your child may not see a teacher until three or four years of age, getting a diagnosis beforehand could reduce the number of interventions or aids your child may need during school-age years. A diagnosis before elementary school can be done by your pediatrician. Schedule an appointment and raise any concerns immediately. Give detailed information explaining exactly what you notice so the pediatrician can either run the appropriate test(s) or direct you to the right specialist.

If your child has already started school—no matter the age—the school is required to conduct a Child Find. The federal Individuals with Disabilities Education Act (IDEA) includes regulations (34 C.F.R. Section 300.111(a)(1)(i)) that require schools to have policies and procedures in place to ensure that all children "who are in need of special education and related services, are identified, located, and evaluated."

Child Find applies to all children residing in any state, even if that child is homeless or is a ward of the state. It also applies to children who are suspected of having a disability or might need special education, even if the child is advancing from grade to grade. The regulatory requirements affect schools because states receive federal funds to assist with paying for education. Schools, therefore, receive federal funds, through their respective state governments, to pay for special education expenses. These expenses include paying teachers, teacher aides, and supplemental materials necessary for instruction. As a result of receiving federal funding, the schools must comply with the federal regulations.

Child Find is significant. Even if you don't suspect a disability in your child, a teacher is legally required to notice it. Once again, the earlier the diagnosis and knowing whether there is a disability, the sooner you can help your child. It's also important to remember that your child may still have a disability even if advancing from one grade to the next. Early diagnosis and an IEP can set your child up to maximize potential, not just get by.

CASE EXAMPLE
(Child Find)

Montuori v. District of Columbia School District

A.M. (minors' names are disguised in court cases) was diagnosed with attention-deficit/hyperactivity disorder (ADHD). A.M. had been under a 504 Service Agreement since elementary school. (This agreement details how a school will provide the necessary supports and remove any barriers so a child can access the general curriculum with their classmates). When A.M. entered middle school, another psychological reevaluation was conducted, and another 504 Service Agreement was implemented. The school wanted to offer a 504 Service Agreement, and conduct a Functional Behavior Assessment (FBA) to address A.M.'s escalating behavioral issues. However, the parents wanted an IEP, so they filed a due process complaint (an IEP allows for additional specialized instruction outside the regular curriculum).[1]

The issue before the court was: Had the school district violated its Child Find obligations by not also evaluating A.M. for an IEP? The court found for the parents, that the school had failed to timely evaluate A.M. for an IEP, thus constituting a Child Find violation. Why?

The answer is because Child Find is an "affirmative obligation," meaning it was a requirement of the school to identify A.M. as a child who may be in need of special education services, and thus should have sent a Permission to Evaluate form to the parents to have the school conduct an evaluation.[2] The school district believed it was relieved of its Child Find obligations when the parents and school officials agreed at a school meeting to proceed with a 504 Plan in lieu of initiating IDEA services. However, the court noted that even if A.M.'s parents had been content with having only the 504 plan, the school should have sought permission from the parents to do the required testing but failed to do so.

---

[1] Full descriptions of 504 Service Agreements and IEPs, and relevant case examples, are in Step Three.
[2] Permission to Evaluate forms are explained in Step Two.

Thought Question:

Do you think your school has violated its Child Find obligations with your child? If so, what evidence do you have? For young children, remember to distinguish between behaviors consistent with other children the same age and behaviors consistent with the disability. These are the factors a court will consider and the school district will use in its defense.

_____

_____

_____

_____

_____

CASE EXAMPLE
(IDEA and "child with a disability")

Durbrow v. Cobb County School District

C.D. was diagnosed with ADHD in third grade. Nevertheless, he advanced from elementary school through to his junior year of high school, and excelled in advanced academic programs and standardized tests. He was admitted into a select magnet school with accelerated courses, where he received accommodations through a 504 plan. His junior-year teachers dismissed the parents' suggestion that C.D. also needed an IEP. Two teachers even wrote him letters of recommendation to attend the Massachusetts Institute of Technology. However, C.D.'s academic performance plummeted his senior year. He amassed late and incomplete work throughout the year, which culminated in five failing grades. The school continued to change his 504 plan with different accommodations, but his grades continued to decline. His parents requested that the school begin the process to evaluate their son for an IEP, and said that C.D. was IDEA-eligible based on his failure to submit his assignments on time. The special education supervisor also believed C.D.'s incomplete work was due to his ADHD, but C.D. himself and his senior-year teachers attributed the failing grades to his procrastination. His parents filed a due process hearing complaint alleging the school district failed in their Child Find obligations. The issue before the court was: Did the IDEA compel the public school district to provide special education to C.D., a student with ADHD, who displayed vast academic potential but struggled to complete his work?

Under the IDEA, a child with a disability is defined as someone with "intellectual disabilities…other health impairments, or specific learning disabilities; and who, by reason thereof, needs special education and related services." One such health impairment is ADHD that adversely affects a child's educational performance. Therefore, to establish entitlement to a FAPE, a student with ADHD must show that the chronic condition adversely affects academic performance, and thus special education is needed.

The court found the school district did not deprive C.D. of a FAPE because he did not need special education and, therefore, did not qualify as a child with a disability. Additionally, the school district did not breach its Child Find obligations because the IDEA requires schools to identify, locate, and evaluate only children with disabilities. The court concluded C.D. was not a child with a disability because he did not, on account of ADHD, require special education; instead, he met or exceeded academic expectations. He had been admitted to a selective magnet program based on his achievements in math and science and had demonstrated college readiness by excelling on the PSAT. Until his senior year, he passed all of his classes in an advanced academic program, including Honors and Advanced Placement courses. Additionally, C.D.'s teachers testified that special education was inappropriate for him, and none attributed his poor grades to low ability. Although C.D. had difficulty with time management and organization, so too did many of his classmates, particularly at the demanding magnet program.

Thought Questions:

Two key questions to consider if you notice failing grades:

1. When did your child's grades start declining?

_____

_____

_____

_____

_____

2. What other reasons could cause your child's grades to decline other than the disability?

_____

_____

_____

_____

_____

Answers to this second question will allow you to take a broader view of issues that you may have overlooked or forgotten, and will also allow you to anticipate the school's response.

Step Two

Why Is an Evaluation Important?

An evaluation will determine if your child has a disability. There are two types of evaluations that can be conducted. One is an **Evaluation Report**, and the other is an **Independent Educational Evaluation** (IEE). You cannot ask for an IEE until an Evaluation Report is completed, and you can only request it if you are not satisfied with the Evaluation Report's results.

The Evaluation Report (ER) is based on tests conducted by the school psychologist, and it will determine whether your child has a disability and whether your child needs special education (an IEP plan) or accommodations for services (a 504 Service Agreement). An ER can take place after the Child Find process.[3]

If a school identifies your child as needing to be evaluated, it will send home a Permission to Evaluate consent form. This form will include the reason(s) of concern for wanting to conduct an evaluation and the tests that will be used during the evaluation.

If your child has not been identified by the school, but you suspect there is a learning disability, you can request an ER. This request can be made verbally or in writing, but I strongly suggest that you put it in writing to begin with, if for no other reason than the school will have to send you a Permission to Evaluate consent form to get the request in writing. Putting the request in writing from the beginning will save time. As importantly, a hard copy gives you documentation for your own records. After the request is made, the school must send home a Permission to Evaluate consent form. If it is not received, follow up with the school. There are no set guidelines on how long the school has to send a parent the consent form. Check your state's rules to determine whether there are state guidelines. (For example, the Pennsylva-

---

[3] See Step One for an explanation of Child Find; see Step Three for a discussion on IEPs and 504 Service Agreements.

nia Department of Education recommends approximately ten days as a best practice to be followed by its schools.)

Remember, this consent form does not provide your child special education services. It only allows the school to test your child to determine whether services are needed. If the school wants to evaluate your child and you do not consent, the school can request a due process hearing to have a hearing officer determine whether it can evaluate your child without your consent. If approved by the hearing officer, the school has sixty calendar days to evaluate your child and complete its report.

If services are recommended, a separate consent form called a Notice of Recommended Educational Placement (NOREP) or Prior Written Consent (PWN), depending on your state, allowing your child to receive services will be provided. If you do not provide consent for the initial provision of special education services, your child cannot and will not receive services. The school cannot force the services upon you by seeking a due process hearing. Federal rules specifically allow for a school to evaluate your child without your permission but prohibits it from enforcing those services. This is why two different forms are required.

Conversely, a school has the right to refuse your request to evaluate your child for special education services. However, the school must put in writing the reason(s) for its refusal. The school's refusal would be documented in the NOREP/PWN. The NOREP/PWN is used any time there is a refusal or any other proposed change to a child's identification, placement, or provision of a Free Appropriate Public Education (FAPE).

After either parental consent or an order from a hearing officer, an evaluation team will test your child. The team could include a certified school psychologist, teachers, and/or learning specialists. The team must also include at least one parent. After the evaluation, two decisions are made: (1) whether the child has a disability that makes learning difficult, and 2) whether, as a result of the disability, special education and supports are needed (that is, an IEP is required). In order to receive special education, the child must meet both requirements—has a learning difficulty due to a disability and the disability requires special education for the child to learn. In other words, your child needs specially designed instruction (SDI) to keep up with classmates receiving regular education.

An IEE can be requested, but only if you believe the school's initial ER is inaccurate. Do you think, for example, the wrong tests were used to conduct the evaluation, the conclusions were wrong, or certain types of tests were not conducted? Do you think the ER does not provide enough information to make a determination about your child's disability and receiving appropriate services? If you have any such concerns, you can request an IEE at the school's expense. As with all such requests, this should be made in writing.

If your school refuses to pay for an IEE, you can request a due process hearing in front of a hearing officer, who would decide whether the school's evaluation was appropriate. If the hearing officer finds that the school's ER was appropriate, which is generally measured by its compliance with federal regulations, you will not be entitled to an IEE at school expense. If the hearing officer finds in your favor, however, the school must pay for an IEE.

It is important to know that if the hearing officer does not find in the school's favor, a school may step up and pay for the IEE, or it may seek a second due process hearing. It will again try to demonstrate that its evaluation was appropriate. I point this out because there can be more than one due process hearing when parents and a school do not agree on the services offered in an IEP.

CASE EXAMPLE
(Methodologies)

Colonial School District v. G.K.

G.K. was a student identified as disabled under the category of autism and needed special education and related services under an IEP. G.K.'s disability was causing learning difficulties, particularly with reading comprehension, written expression, math problem solving, and both social language and social skills. The parents requested in writing that the school district not promote G.K. to fifth grade because they believed he should obtain mastery at the fourth-grade level before being presented with higher-level work. The school district denied the request, stating that school data and anecdotal information showed that G.K. had made excellent improvement both academically and socially. Additionally, G.K. was turning twelve, and the school did not think it would be appropriate or beneficial for him to be two years older than his classmates. When their request was denied, G.K.'s parents filed a due process complaint.[4] At mediation, the parents and school district agreed to advance G.K. to the fifth grade, and the parents would be provided with the overall school's Benchmark Assessment, which was conducted to see how children were doing comparatively. They would need this to assess their son's status in relation to other students in his grade. The school district also agreed to pay for an IEE. The Benchmark Assessment results showed that G.K. functioned at an Advanced or Proficient level in some areas, but only at a Basic level in other areas. In some instances, he was at the Below Basic level.

The evaluator hired for the IEE used the Wechsler Individual Achievement Test. Results showed that G.K. functioned in the Average or Above Average range in most of the subtests, but was Below Average in reading comprehension and oral expression. Based on this, the school district revised G.K.'s IEP. Even so, his parents remained concerned about the identified deficiencies from the school's Benchmark Assessment, and how they were going to be addressed. His parents filed for a due process hearing.

---

[4] How to file a complaint is described in Step Four, as is a definition of mediation.

At the hearing, the parents explained that that the standards of assessment built into G.K.'s IEP were not linked to any consistent or objective testing. It appeared to them that apparent success could be obtained by giving G.K. easier material in class; without objective testing, there was no way to determine if he was actually moving forward. The question before the court was: Did G.K.'s parents have a right to determine the method the school district used to measure progress on meeting G.K.'s IEP goals?

The court ruled that they did not have this right. How was this decision reached? The court acknowledged it was possible that, despite disagreement by the school district, the method one parent had outlined for progress measurement was feasible and even desirable. However, there was no legal obligation that the school had to use it. This is not a requirement of a FAPE. Additionally, there was no evidence that the school district had failed to comply with any of the guarantees of parental participation in the IDEA and its regulations. The parents had fully participated; disagreeing with the results did not matter. The due process complaint did not indicate that the parents did not comprehend the IEP or found it confusing in any respect. Instead, the parents wrote that goals and objectives in the IEP were dubious and inadequate and did not address the core needs of their child.

Thus, the issue in this case was dissatisfaction on the part of G.K.'s parents with how progress was measured. To get to this conclusion, the court reiterated that the measure and adequacy of an IEP can only be determined at the time it is offered to the student, not in hindsight at a later date. In G.K.'s case, he had improved both academically and socially under the measurements being used by the school, even though he had not met the proposed goals.

Note: If your child is determined to have a disability but does not need special education or an SDI, it is still possible your child is eligible to receive support or accommodations in school through a 504 Service Agreement.[1]

---

1 See Step Three for more about 504 Service Agreements.

CASE EXAMPLE
(Reevaluations and IEEs)

N.D.S. v. Academy for Science and Agriculture Charter School (ASACS)

Based on the court records, N.D.S. was initially evaluated in the first grade (the year was not included in the court decision) and was found to qualify for special education and related services, and the last reevaluation occurred in 2011. When N.D.S. started attending ASACS in 2013, the school conducted its own reevaluation to ensure she was receiving the necessary services. The IEP team completed the evaluation in February 2014, and there was no indication that her parents disagreed with it. However, after N.D.S. experienced some physical and emotional challenges, her parents requested a reevaluation, to which the school agreed. The reevaluation was completed in December 2015, and again the parents did not disagree with it.

N.D.S. suffered a concussion in June 2017 that caused her physical symptoms and learning difficulties to worsen. N.D.S.'s doctor recommended that her parents meet with the IEP team to develop an updated IEP; they did not. Instead, the parents wrote an email in late October 2017 outlining why they thought the December 2015 reevaluation was inadequate and requested an IEE. The school refused to pay for an IEE, instead offering to reevaluate N.D.S. The parents filed a due process complaint.

The issue before the court was: Could N.D.S.'s parents refuse to allow the school to reevaluate their daughter in order to get an IEE paid for by the school? The ruling was no, the parents could not do this.

It's important to remember that the IEP process begins with an initial full evaluation to determine whether the child is entitled to special education and related services. The child's parents have a right to a copy of the evaluation and, if they disagree with the evaluation, then have the right to request an IEE at the school's expense. Generally, a school is required to reevaluate a child at least once every three years and is not required to pay for an IEE unless the parent disagrees with the evaluation.

The court explained that in this case, the IDEA and its implementing regulations make the purpose of the IEE clear: a school has an obligation to do an evaluation; if a parent disagrees with the results, the school must defend the adequacy of the evaluation at a hearing; if the school is unwilling to do so, the school must pay for an IEE. The purpose of conducting an IEE is to address the matter in controversy, which is the specific alleged shortcomings in the school's evaluation.

N.D.S.'s parents wanted to circumvent the reevaluation and thus minimize the role that the school played in the reevaluation process. Everyone involved in this case agreed that the December 2015 reevaluation had become obsolete in light of the concussion N.D.S. suffered during summer 2017. The school wanted to do a reevaluation so that it could propose changes to the IEP to meet her current needs. By N.D.S.'s parents refusing to allow the school to reevaluate her, they were expressing disagreement with the accuracy of the December 2015 reevaluation. This would force the school to either defend the two-year-old evaluation as accurate or pay for an IEE. The court considered this outcome to be far removed from the cooperative process that the US Supreme Court had identified as the core of IDEA. The court considered the parents' actions as undermining the process, finding that they cannot simply disagree with a past evaluation, refuse to allow a reevaluation with no explanation, and then demand an IEE that is ultimately paid for by taxpayers.

Note: If your school agrees to pay for an IEE, you will be required to find the evaluator. To be able to compare apples to apples, it's important to make sure that the person hired has the same or similar credentials as the school psychologist and that the evaluation would use the same criteria as the school's initial evaluation. Information on the criteria the school used in its evaluation can be obtained from the school. If the school refuses to pay, you can still hire an evaluator but at your own cost. Check with your insurance company to determine whether and to what extent this would be covered, and if there is a required copayment.

The answers to the following may allow you to effectively challenge a school district's assessment. Keep in mind, though, that courts generally defer to school districts and prefer not to override a district's authority, especially when it comes to testing because there is an assumption schools know best. Schools are in the business of educating and knowing about education methodology. Courts are in the business of knowing the law, and hearing officials and judges want to keep it that way.

Thought Questions:

1. If your child needs an IEE, are the school and private evaluator using different tests? If so, which tests are being used? As a parent, you need to learn the differences among tests and what symptoms or disabilities they test for.

___

2. If the school and private evaluator are using different tests, why is one test being used over another test?

___

3. If your private evaluator is not using the same test the school used, ask why/why not?

___

4. If your private evaluator is familiar with the test used by the school but using a different test, ask: What are the pros and cons of each?

_____
_____
_____
_____
_____

5. Are the assessments testing for the same symptoms of a disability but using different methodologies, or are they testing for completely different symptoms (and perhaps a different disability)?

_____
_____
_____
_____
_____

6. Is one type of testing more or less detailed than another?

_____
_____
_____
_____
_____

CASE EXAMPLE
(Expert Comparisons)

B.G. v. Illinois State Board of Education

B.G. was diagnosed with a specific learning disability and also had significant behavior and attendance issues. His living situation alternated between living with his mother who only spoke Spanish and living with his father. His father was so much of an absentee parent that B.G. was left to his own devices when he lived with him. B.G. repeated the first grade and would have repeated the seventh grade, but the school district promoted him due to his age. He was absent for one-third of the 2013–14 school year when he was in seventh grade. After B.G.'s father died in April 2014, B.G. was hospitalized with diagnoses of morbid obesity, hypertension, severe hypoxia syndrome, Type 2 diabetes, and obstructive sleep apnea. In July 2014, B.G.'s mother filed a request for a due process hearing with the Illinois State Board of Education, alleging a violation of the IDEA and a denial of FAPE. The parties mediated (mediator names are never included in court cases) the claim in August, with the result being that B.G. was assigned an aide and moved to a classroom with a teacher familiar with multisensory approaches to teaching, reading, and writing for students with dyslexia. Around the same time, the district began to perform psychological assessments of B.G.'s educational needs that would wind up at the center of the case. The results of the assessments were presented at an October 2014 IEP meeting, at which B.G.'s mother did not voice any objections to the ER. Nevertheless, she felt there were issues with it, and requested an IEE at the school's expense in seven study areas. The district requested a due process hearing to defend its results and not fund an IEE; B.G.'s mother located an outside psychiatrist to testify.

The hearing officer found the district's witnesses credible and persuasive, and discounted the testimony of B.G.'s expert because the person lacked Illinois certifications and had never met B.G. The hearing officer concluded that the school district had carried out its burden to show that its evaluations were appropriate. B.G.'s mother then filed motions in a federal district court to supplement the administrative record and reverse the hearing officer's decision.

The issue before the district court was: Was B.G. entitled to a school-funded IEE when issues with the Evaluation Report, according to the court, were minor? The court ruled against the mother.

The court pointed out that two school psychologists conducted the district's psychological assessment of B.G. One psychologist administered two assessments before going on maternity leave, and the other psychologist interpreted the data. The second psychologist reviewed B.G.'s academic history, previous evaluations, and medical history; and also performed classroom observations in B.G.'s general education class and in his special education classroom. The court decided that the record contained substantial evidence that the psychologists had sufficient knowledge, training, and experience to administer assessments. The court was also unwilling to fault the hearing officer for discounting the testimony of B.G.'s expert, who claimed that the school's psychologists should have used different methods. The second school psychologist knew B.G., while the outside expert (also a psychologist) had never met or evaluated him. It was, thus, understandable that the hearing officer thought the second school psychologist's explanation was more persuasive.

B.G.'s mother claimed the two school psychologists ignored her son's potential ADHD in their evaluations. The court, however, noted that ADHD is a medical diagnosis that can only be made by a medical professional and is thus outside the area of expertise of the school evaluators. Without a medical diagnosis, there was nothing the district's school psychologists could have done differently, and they were not licensed to make a medical diagnosis during their evaluations.

Note: School psychologists are generally certified and regulated by your state's department of education. For example, the qualifications to be a certified school psychologist in Pennsylvania include having at least a bachelor's degree (although advanced degrees, such as a masters in art or in education or a doctorate degree are more common); having completed one thousand hours of supervised practice; and passing the PRAXIS exam.

Private child psychologists are also licensed through the state but generally from a different state agency. For example, in Pennsylvania, child psychologists are licensed by Pennsylvania's Department of State's Bureau of Professional and Occupational Affairs and are regulated by the Pennsylvania Board of Psychology. Again, by way of example, the qualifications to be a private child psychologist in Pennsylvania, with some exceptions, generally includes having a doctoral degree from a university accredited by the American Psychological Association; having two full years of supervised practice; passing both state and national examinations; being declared of good moral character; not having committed a felony; and completing thirty hours of continuing education every two years to maintain a license.

If your child has been given a medical diagnosis of a disability from a licensed child psychologist, that does not automatically mean special education services will be provided. A medical diagnosis is just one part of the process. A school still needs its own team, called a multidisciplinary team, to determine the child's educational classification. A multidisciplinary team would include a certified school psychologist, who would consider the findings and diagnoses from a licensed child psychologist in making a determination about receiving an SDI.

CASE EXAMPLE
(Weighing Credibility of Experts)

Y.N. v. Board of Education of the Harrison Central School District

S.N. was a child with a disability who underwent a private psycho-educational evaluation and an audiological evaluation. The diagnoses were a learning disorder with impairment in reading, ADHD, an unspecified anxiety disorder, and a central auditory processing disorder. S.N.'s public school developed an IEP for her. The parents hired an outside psychologist to conduct a neuropsychological evaluation of S.N. to assess her cognitive, academic, and social-emotional functioning, and to assist in ongoing educational and treatment planning. The doctor made six educational recommendations, and the parents chose to place S.N. in a private school, not the public school, and then sought tuition reimbursement from the school district. The district agreed on a settlement that included allowing it to conduct reasonable observations of S.N. and to be provided with the results of all evaluations conducted thus far. The school district also conducted its own reevaluation, which included a psychological evaluation and a speech/language evaluation. It recommended a new IEP for S.N., but the parents disagreed with the conclusions of the school's reevaluation and its IEP. The parents contended that:

> *They were denied meaningful participation in the development of the IEP and the [doctor's] opinion that [S.N.] requires full-time special education program was completely disregarded at the meeting; the resource room recommendation was not appropriate to meet [S.N.'s] significant educational needs and would cause her to miss special classes she enjoys; the CSE [Committee on Special Education] failed to conduct a social history and a structured observation of [S.N.]; the characterization of [S.N.'s] disability as mild was incorrect; there was incorrect reporting of [S.N.'s] scores on the speech/language evaluation*

and educational evaluation; and there was reliance on the school psychologist's evaluation, which refers to an incorrect birthdate for [S.N.]; the mistakes are examples of the CSE's misunderstanding of [S.N.'s] complex needs which resulted in a minimal program recommendation, immeasurable goals, and classroom accommodations that cannot be implemented throughout the day.

The question before the court was: Should a privately retained expert who performed an evaluation and rendered a different conclusion than the school's expert be given more credibility? As above, the court's answer here was it should not. Under the IDEA, "a CSE [must] actually review evaluative data and base the terms of the student's IEP on that information." This includes an IEE obtained by a parent at private expense. It is a school's responsibility to demonstrate which evaluative materials were reviewed during the CSE meeting in reaching the terms of the IEP. In this case, the IEP explicitly stated that "all evaluations were reviewed." For each description of S.N.'s functional performance and learning characteristics, the committee cited the test or evaluation on which it was basing its decisions. The parents argued that the committee did not adopt, or at least give enough credence to, their outside expert's recommendations. However, the CSE was not required to do so, and therefore it had not committed a procedural violation of the IDEA. The committee was not required to accept the recommendations merely because the doctor was an expert.

Note: An additional and frequently cited reason given by judges is that courts tend to defer to school districts' recommendations for educational programming over privately retained experts.

CASE EXAMPLE
(Rights of Parents)

In Luo v. Owen J. Roberts School District

Luo is the father of B.L., a minor who was receiving special education. B.L. was originally placed in a day program, but Luo later asked that his child be moved to a residential program. The IEP team agreed to the request. After meeting with the special education supervisor, however, Luo received a revised IEP indicating that B.L. was ineligible for such placement. The revised IEP also included an SDI directing Luo to take a parent-training course, to which he filed a due process complaint.

The school district also paid for and conducted an IEE, after which the IEP team proposed an additional revision to the IEP: a recommendation of a behavioral specialist to observe B.L. at school and at home. Luo agreed to this.

After the adaptive behavior evaluation, the specialist concluded that B.L. was more independent at school than at home, and also recommended that Luo undergo parent training. The school district issued a Notice of Recommended Educational Placement notifying Luo of its intent to implement the proposed SDI requiring parent training. Luo again filed a request for a due process hearing. The question before the hearing officer was: Had Luo (the father) been deprived of his right to informed consent when he did not give consent to the specific methodology used by the behavioral specialist? The answer was that Luo's rights were not deprived.

This case was analyzed using the United States Constitution. There are, of course, numerous rights we hold as US citizens, but the rights protected have to be fundamental rights; or, as the court put it, "Such rights reflect basic values implicit in the concept of ordered liberty such that neither liberty nor justice would exist if they were sacrificed." In this case, Luo had consented to having an assessment made by the behavioral specialist, but he did not have a constitutionally protected interest in being advised of the methodology to be used. This was not the sort of "fundamental" interest entitled to the protection of the US Constitution.

Note: This case takes another look at parental rights but from a different angle. Parents have no legal right to a specific methodology by way of any federal statute or the Constitution.

CASE EXAMPLE
(New Disability Diagnosis)

M.B. v. City School District of New Rochelle

R.A.B. had several medical conditions, including hydrocephalus, macrocephaly, epilepsy, cerebral palsy, and spastic dysplasia. R.A.B. received special education services beginning in kindergarten. Before his transition to middle school, the school district conducted a reevaluation in May 2013 to prepare a new IEP for the 2013–14 school year. His parents expressed concern that R.A.B.'s current program was not making a difference and he was not making academic progress.

The team created a comprehensive IEP for the new school year, which included a suite of special educational services, including placement in special class scheduling, adapted physical education, bilingual speech therapy, occupational therapy, physical therapy, home-based programming of individual therapy, a shared aide for two hours a day, extended school year services (i.e., into the summer) and door-to-door transportation with a matron. At the end of the school year in May 2014, the parents and the IEP team reconvened to create a new IEP for the 2014–15 school year. They repeated their concerns that R.A.B. had not shown academic progress; worse was that he had regressed regarding his independent living skills. The teacher also noted R.A.B.'s inability to progress academically without 1:1 supervision. As a result, the 2014–15 comprehensive IEP included services that were similar to the prior IEP but with changes to the shared aide. In the newest IEP, a shared aide was provided on a daily basis as needed; assistive technology was available, including an iPad with access to assistive technology software; and an assistive technology consultation would be conducted every two weeks. The parents also paid for a private neurodevelopment IEE on R.A.B. that they submitted to the school. The evaluation concluded that R.A.B. met the criteria for a diagnosis of autism. Based on this evaluation, the parents requested a 1:1 aide and an out-of-school-district program.

The IEP team met in May 2015 and developed a new IEP for the 2015–16 school year. The team rejected the out-of-school-district program, and instead offered the same special educational services as the 2014–15 plan but increased the shared aide to "throughout the school day" (as opposed to as needed, but not 1:1 as the parents requested), access to water, and a safety plan because R.A.B. had fallen at school. The parents did not approve of the IEP and filed a due process complaint.

The question before the court was: Had R.A.B. been denied a FAPE for school years 2013–14, 2014–15, and 2015–16? The court ruled yes, but only for the 2015–16 school, in large part because the school had not acknowledged the new autism diagnosis and the IEP was "largely the same as that of the previous year."

The court analyzed whether the IEP allowed for meaningful benefit.[5] A school district fulfills its substantive obligations under the IDEA if it provides an IEP that is likely to produce progress, not regression, and if it affords the student opportunities for real educational benefits. The record demonstrated that from February to May 2013, the school district had produced the following reports or conducted the following evaluations on R.A.B.:

- an occupational therapy annual report;
- a physical therapy annual report;
- a home-based Applied Behavioral Analysis progress report;
- a social history update;
- an educational evaluation;
- a psychological evaluation;

---

5 Again, for more on this term, see the section titled "Post the Endrew F. Case" at the end of this book

- a bilingual speech/language evaluation; and
- a medical evaluation.

Although R.A.B. was not specifically evaluated for autism or assistive technology, a subcommittee of the CSE had enough information regarding R.A.B.'s social and emotional conditions to develop a current IEP that addressed his individual needs. In other words, the performed evaluations were "sufficiently comprehensive to identify all of the student's special education needs," even if they weren't sufficient to identify the underlying causes. Simply put, there was no showing that the autism-specific evaluation (i.e., the formal autism diagnosis) would have changed the school's recommended suite of special education services. As a result, there was no basis for the court to conclude that any procedural violations that may have occurred resulted in denial of a FAPE prior to the 2015–16 school year.

Thought Questions:

1. Is your child's IEP likely to produce progress as it is written?

2. How does your definition of progress compare with the school's definition?

3. Did your child previously exhibit behaviors related to a later diagnosis? If so, what were they?

Step Three

What Is an IEP Versus a 504 Service Agreement?

This step explains the difference between an IEP and a 504 Service Agreement. First up is the IEP.

IEP is the acronym for Individualized Education Program. An IEP is drafted by an IEP team. That team must include the parent(s), at least one regular education teacher if your child will be in a regular education classroom, at least one special education teacher, school psychologist, and any other specialist your child may need or use, such as a speech or hearing therapist. Your child may also attend the IEP meetings but is not required to do so.

It is the school district's responsibility to ensure your presence at IEP meetings, or at least to ensure you have the opportunity to participate. It must notify you early enough to schedule the meeting at a time and place agreed upon by all the parties. Meeting notices sent out by the school should include the time and location, its purpose, who will be in attendance, and notification that other specialists can also participate. If you would like to participate but cannot physically be present, the district should allow for other methods of participation, including conference calls. If you refuse to attend, the meeting can proceed without you.

The IEP team must make numerous considerations when developing the IEP, including your child's strengths and weaknesses and academic, developmental, and functional needs, as well as your concerns as the parent. If you or a member of the IEP team believes changes at a later date are needed, agreed-upon changes can be made. The IEP can be changed entirely or individual amendments can be made. The IEP must be reviewed no less than annually; however, parents can request a meeting with the IEP team for a review sooner if they feel it is necessary.

An IEP should explain whether your child will participate with nondisabled children in a regular classroom setting. When it comes to tests, it's important to remember that disabled children will still be required to participate in state and district assessments. Accordingly, if your child will have accommodations to assist in taking these assessments, information about the accommodations must be provided. If your child will be taking a different type of assessment other than the standard test, an explanation must be provided explaining the reason(s) why and the name of the alternate test. Last, the IEP must state when the services can be expected to begin and their frequency, location, and duration.

An IEP is a written plan for a child with a disability who also needs SDI. That plan should include information about the child's current academic achievement, the specific disability, and how the disability affects educational development. The IEP should also include *measurable* annual goals that meet your child's needs and ensures continued academic progress despite the disability. Having measurable goals is key because your child may not succeed if the IEP is too general or vague. To guard against this, make sure the IEP provides: a description of how progress will be measured; when periodic reports on that progress will be provided; and criterion that are measurable, reasonable, and consistent.

The following are examples of valid, positive measurable goals.

- "When it's time to begin an assignment..."
- "When the teacher asks for an answer to a question..."

This describes when or under what conditions the behavior will take place.

- "[Student] will complete assignments using a No. 2 pencil."

This describes what the student will use to perform the behavior.

- "[Student] will...in the cafeteria..." (or in the library, in the reading classroom, on the school bus, etc.).

This describes where the behavior will occur.

- "On 3 out of 4 occasions..."
- "15% of math time..."

"2 on a scale of 1 to 5, with 5 being the highest level of achievement..."
This describes the measurement to be used on performance criteria.

- "[Student] will have 85% correct over 3 consecutive tests."

This includes your child's name as the person who will be doing the behavior.

The following are negative examples because the goals are vague.

- "[Student] will understand numbers."
- "[Student] will know spelling words."
- "[Student] will recognize materials."
- "[Student] will behave in class."
- "[Student] will comprehend what is said."
- "[Student] will improve speech.

    These goals are not measurable. For example, what does it mean to "understand" numbers? Does that mean your child will recognize them, or does it mean your child will know how to count? There is no specificity as to what exactly is meant or how that goal will be met.

    Think about it like this. In your job, you have duties, responsibilities, expectations, and goals. To maximize your opportunity to get a raise or promotion, you must have measurable goals to demonstrate quantifiable results. This information provides baseline date from which you can measure. Your child's IEP should be treated the same way. Having measurable goals will produce quantifiable results and data, and thus you and the IEP team can better gauge whether your child is improving, regressing, or remaining stagnant. Data is key, and the school should be keeping a record of it. If the school does not provide it, you should make a request to see it.

CASE EXAMPLE
(IEP supports and FAPE)

Carr v. New Glarus School District

S.C. suffered a traumatic brain injury in December 2010, and the resulting disability made him eligible to receive special education and related services.

By 2015 S.C. began the school year as a junior in the school district that had developed an IEP for him. After the first week, however, the parents requested, and were allowed, to transfer S.C. to the New Glarus School District. At the time, the new district also accepted the August 2015 IEP created by the old school district. That IEP provided that S.C. would participate full-time with nondisabled peers in regular education classes but would also receive special education services for fifteen minutes once a week. The special education services were described in the IEP as "academic self-management" that focused on teaching S.C. study skills and following up with organization and prioritization. The IEP further provided for multiple services and aids related to math assessments, organizational assistance, reminders, extended timelines for assignment completion, and retaking summative assessments. The IEP did not, however, require any teacher or staff to verify the accuracy of S.C.'s self-reporting of missing and completed assignments; to check his grades and assignments on the school intranet; to consult with other teachers to determine if S.C.'s grades were lower than expected due to incomplete rubrics; or to consult with other teachers about working with S.C. on study strategies.

S.C. was enrolled in a precalculus math class that used the College Preparatory Math methodology; this class had just five students. In the first trimester, he began with a grade of D but ended with a grade of C+. Even so, his parents were concerned about his math grade and his ability to take calculus as a senior. They requested that S.D. be allowed to take a math class in yet another district. The New Glarus School District did not respond to this request. The parents and the New Glarus IEP team then had a meeting, and while the IEP was revised, there was no mention of math in another school district. The revised IEP was never implemented because the parents requested a formal facilitated meeting with the Wisconsin Special Education Mediation System. When that did not proceed as the parents wanted, they filed a due process complaint.[6]

The question before the hearing officer was: Had the New Glarus School District failed to provide a FAPE by not offering S.D. a math class appropriate to meet his needs and by not implementing various provisions of his IEP?

The parents argued that S.C. could not learn using a certain deductive reasoning style required by the school, and that is what denied him a FAPE. However, the hearing officer ruled in the school's favor because S.C. actually had made progress. Additionally, the hearing officer recognized that precalculus was a notoriously challenging class for a regular education student, and S.C.'s improved grade was a clear indicator that his learning had improved.

The parents then appealed to a federal court, which assessed S.C.'s progress to determine whether a FAPE had been denied. The court also ruled for the school district because S.C. had made some progress in his math class. While the court acknowledged that the IDEA required school districts to provide children with disabilities with a FAPE in the least restrictive environment, the statuary directive did not require the school district to educate disabled children to their highest potential. Instead, the education provided needed to be sufficient to confer some educational benefit. Specific to this case, the court considered that the school district was allowed discretion in determining what S.C.'s IEP should entail, and how, if at all, it should be revised midstream.

---

[6] How to file a complaint is discussed in Step Four.

Thought Question:

1. Has your child made academic progress in a class? If so, what has been the progress? What is the academic rigor of that class, generally speaking?

_____

_____

_____

_____

_____

CASE EXAMPLE
(IEP supports and Behavioral Disability)

Smith v. District of Columbia School District

A.J. has emotional disturbance that leads to frequent emotional dysregulation and behavioral issues. In school he has frequent conflicts with peers and teachers, and physical altercations occur two to three times per week. These emotional disturbances also interfere with his education. In fall 2015, at the beginning of A.J.'s freshman year in high school, his IEP indicated that he required a self-contained environment in order to succeed academically and behaviorally. It also provided for 26.5 hours per week of specialized instruction outside the general education setting. A.J. was initially placed in the Specific Learning Support program, which was designed for students with learning disabilities, even though he has an emotional disability, not a learning disability.

After more fights with students, A.J. was moved from the Specific Learning Support program to the Behavior and Education Support program, which provides full-time instruction outside the general education setting with supports for students with emotional disabilities. A month later, his mother requested that A.J. be evaluated for placement in general education Advanced Placement courses. When she was informed that the hours on A.J.'s IEP would have to be reduced for him to attend these types of classes, she declined to forfeit the hours. Thus, A.J. did not receive any advanced curriculum.

A.J.'s mother filed a due process complaint against the school district alleging that the initial placement in the Specific Learning Support program had been inappropriate and amounted to a denial of a FAPE. The issue to be decided was: Had the school district denied a FAPE to A.J., who is intellectually gifted but limited in accessing general education by his emotional disturbance, by placing him in a program designed for children with specific learning disabilities? The court agreed with the mother that the Specific Learning Support program was not tailored to A.J.'s needs and that it failed to provide him with personally challenging objectives. The IEP explicitly described how A.J.'s emotional disturbance hindered his ability to learn, and the Specific Learning Support program did not meet his needs because it was designed to accommodate children with learning disabilities, not emotional disabilities.

In this case, the hearing officer at the due process hearing acknowledged that the IEP did not explicitly mandate placement in the Behavior and Education Support program. However, the court also acknowledged that the IEP plainly included that a self-contained classroom environment would address A.J.'s emotional disturbance issues, and made clear that he required this environment in order to succeed academically and behaviorally.

CASE EXAMPLE
(IEP and transportation)

E.I.H. v. Fair Lawn Board of Education

L.H., who had been diagnosed with autism, attended an out-of-school-district placement. Her IEP included transportation to and from the school as a "related service." After L.H. had a seizure, she was also diagnosed with epilepsy and prescribed Diastat, a medication that must be administered rectally for seizures lasting longer than two minutes. The school district contemplated whether to add a nurse-transportation component to the IEP, but instead added nursing services to L.H.'s individualized health plan. This decision was made because the IEP team decided the potential need for Diastat was responding to a medical issue, not an educational one. However, not adding a nurse-transportation component to the IEP meant L.H. would not have a nurse with her on the bus rides to and from school to administer a prescribed medication. Her parents filed a due process claim saying this was a violation of the IDEA.

The hearing officer ruled in favor of the parents because L.H.'s physician had concluded that L.H. needed a nurse on the bus as a part of her transportation-related service, so the district was required to amend the IEP. The hearing officer ordered the district to pay the parents $192 as compensation for previously transporting their daughter to and from school until the accompanying medical professional was provided.

The parents then brought an action in federal court to recover their attorney's fees. To determine the reimbursement, the court considered again: Was there a denial of a FAPE when the school district denied a nurse on the bus yet bus transportation was included in an IEP as a related service, and L.H. needed a nurse on the bus in the event of a seizure? The district court reversed the administrative hearing officer's finding and ruled that the inclusion of the nurse on the bus was not a "related service" and necessary to enable a FAPE. The parents appealed again to the federal 3rd circuit, the appellate court explained that as a general rule, nursing services are required as a related service through an IEP to the extent such services are designed to enable a child with a disability to receive a FAPE as described in the IEP. Transportation to and from school is deemed a required related service in an IEP if the service is necessary for the student to access and obtain educational benefits. Transportation services can include aides, equipment, assistive devices, or any accommodations as needed. In this case, the court recognized that the record reflected that L.H. could not take the bus, a FAPE-required service, until a nurse was provided to administer the Diastat if needed. As a result, then, a nurse on the bus was necessary for L.H. to gain access to a FAPE, and this should have been included in her IEP, not her individualized health plan.

Thought Questions:

1. How is your child's IEP exactly worded? For example, if your child has a behavior disability (such as with A.J.), what specific language in the IEP addresses these behavioral challenges?

_____

_____

_____

_____

_____

2. If your child has an intellectual disability (such as those in the Specific Learning Support program in A.J.'s school), what specific language in the IEP addresses these intellectual challenges?

_____

_____

_____

_____

_____

3. By statute, transportation is a required related service. Does your child require an aid or nurse on the bus (as did L.H.)? If so, what specific language in the IEP addresses this need?

_____

_____

_____

_____

_____

CASE EXAMPLE
(Specialists at IEP meetings)

Pottsgrove School District v. D.H.

D.H. is an elementary school student diagnosed with autism, and thus is eligible for special education services under the categories of emotional disturbance and speech/language impairment. D.H. is prone to emotional outbursts that sometimes include violent behavior, including throwing furniture and pulling hair. He also struggles with toileting issues. From kindergarten through the second grade, D.H. attended a public school where his academic achievement was at or above grade level, but his behavior suffered. During his three years, school personnel physically restrained him over twenty-five times, including one incident in which personnel called the police. D.H. had at least forty-three toileting accidents, and while his IEP had a behavior plan, it but did not directly address these issues. When he was in kindergarten, the IEP team met to revise his education plan, but neither a behavior specialist nor a Board Certified Behavior Analyst participated. From January to June 2014, D.H. had no less than eighteen toileting accidents, was physically restrained six times, and was picked up early from school fifteen times. The IEP from kindergarten carried over into the first grade, but the IEP team did not reconvene until April 2015. During the first seven months of first grade, D.H. had seated restraints used on him ten times, had thirteen toileting accidents, and behavioral issues that necessitated early departure from school roughly once a week. D.H.'s personal care assistant responded to his behavior with redirection, which was in contravention of the behavior plan. In second grade, his violent outbursts and toileting accidents continued, and he again had to be restrained. The IEP team revised his behavior plan in November and December 2015. In December, D.H.'s mother asked for a formal reevaluation of her son's status to consider transferring him to a program outside the school district; the reevaluation included a Functional Behavior Assessment (FBA). It showed that D.H. still exhibited problem behaviors, so in April 2016 the school district agreed that he be transferred to an approved private school. With the transfer, D.H. improved his behavior and had fewer toileting issues.

The mother filed a due process complaint over his attendance at the public school. The hearing officer ruled in her favor, finding that the Pottsgrove School District had denied D.H. a FAPE during his time at the elementary school. The hearing officer made this ruling because of the absence of important voices during some of the IEP meetings and because of inadequate behavior plans in D.H.'s IEPs. The school district appealed the hearing officer's decision to federal court.

One issue the court had to address on an appeal: Who is required to attend an IEP meeting versus who is allowed to attend an IEP meeting? When faced with the question of whether the school had failed D.H. by not having various specialists at IEP meetings, the hearing officer faulted the school district for not including a behavior specialist, speech/language therapist, occupational therapist, and physical therapist at several of the meetings. In comparison, however, the court ruled that such participants are not required under the IDEA, and it appeared that neither the mother nor school district exercised their statutory discretion to include such members in the IEP meetings.

Note: The IDEA does not require any specific ways to address a student's behaviors, and an FBA is not listed among the statutory components of an IEP. Specifically, the statute reads that "nothing in this section shall be construed to require that additional information be included in a child's IEP beyond what is explicitly required in this section." Therefore, an FBA is an option, not a hard-and-fast requirement. There is also no requirement that any specific person conduct an FBA. Some states, however, allow for greater protection for children with behavioral disabilities through the state's laws or regulations. Regardless, simply because there is no requirement within the IDEA does not mean specialists cannot attend the meetings.

Thought Questions:

1. Who comprises your child's IEP team? What are their names, titles, and responsibilities?

_____

_____

_____

_____

_____

2. Does your child require any additional specialists? If so, have you or the school requested their presence? If yes, do they attend the IEP meetings; and what are their name(s), title(s), and responsibility(ies)? (Remember, the court in D.H.'s case noted that specialists are not required members of an IEP team, but the school and/or D.H.'s mother could have requested their presence, but did not.)

_____

_____

_____

_____

_____

Now let's discuss what is a 504 Service Agreement. A 504 Service Agreement is regulated under the Rehabilitation Act of 1973, which was created as a part of the American with Disabilities Act (ADA). As such, 504 Service Agreements are regulated under the ADA, a civil rights law, whereas IEPs are regulated under the IDEA, an education law.

Officially, Section 504 of the Rehabilitation Act of 1973, is designed to eliminate discrimination on the basis of a handicap in any program or activity receiving federal financial assistance. A handicapped person includes anyone with a physical or mental impairment that *substantially limits one or more major life activities*. A physical or mental impairment has been defined to include any (1) physiological disorder or condition, (2) cosmetic disfigurement, or (3) anatomical loss that affects one or more of the following body systems: neurological; musculoskeletal; special sense organs; respiratory, including speech organs; cardiovascular; reproductive; digestive; genito-urinary; hemic and lymphatic; skin; and endocrine.

It also includes any mental or psychological disorder, such as (1) mental retardation, (2) organic brain syndrome, (3) emotional or mental illness, and (4) specific learning disabilities.

Major life activities include caring for one's self, performing manual tasks, walking, seeing, hearing, speaking, breathing, working, and learning.

So, what does all of this mean? It means if your child has a diagnosed disability but the school has told you there is no need for an SDI (i.e., an IEP) under federal law, the school must still make accommodations if that disability is affecting your child's major life activity, such as learning.

CASE EXAMPLE
(Recording Devices)

Pollack v. Regional School Unit

B.P. was a nineteen-year old student who attended public high school. He had been diagnosed with several disabilities, including autism, cognitive impairment, and a variant of LandauKleffner Syndrome. He was nonverbal and thus unable to communicate with his parents about his experiences at school. His parents wanted him to carry an audio-recording device at school to record everything said in his presence. The school district refused to permit the device, so his parents filed a lawsuit alleging a violation of the ADA.

The issue before the court was: By rejecting the parents' request to equip their son with a recording device, had the school district denied B.P. the benefits of the school's services, programs, or activities or otherwise discriminated against him? The court found the school had not denied benefits or discriminated. This case was analyzed under the ADA, which seeks to eliminate discrimination against all individuals with disabilities. The statute mandates that qualified individuals with a disability shall not, by reason of their disability, be excluded from participation in or be denied the benefits of the services, programs, or activities of a public entity, or be subjected to discrimination by any such entity. This protection is characterized as a guarantee of meaningful access to government benefits and programs. The effective communications regulation requires public entities to "ensure that communications with applicants, participants, members of the public, and companions with disabilities are as effective as communications with others. To achieve this, public entities shall furnish appropriate auxiliary aids and services where necessary to afford individuals with disabilities an equal opportunity to participate in, and enjoy the benefits of, a service program, or activity of a public entity."

Thus, B.P.'s parents' pursuit of an accommodation-based claim of discrimination under the ADA should have included proof of the effectiveness of the proposed accommodation. In other words, the accommodation had to provide B.P. a benefit of increased access to a public service, which in this case was school.

The court pointed out that there had been only a handful of incidents of concern to the parents, and the parents had stated that they felt their son was safe at school. This indicated that the need for a recording device was not a safety issue. The school and parents agreed that B.P. had been making good progress in his educational program, so he was receiving a FAPE. Thus, it was unnecessary for him to wear a recording device to benefit his education.

The court found that allowing B.P. to wear an audio or video device to school that would record his day would instead interfere with his ability to receive FAPE. This was based on previous evidence from both educators and the parent of another child with autism that the recording device was disruptive and detrimental to the education of the student and interfered with the learning process. B.P.'s parents failed to provide any evidence that their son was not receiving a FAPE or to support the assertion that wearing a recording device could benefit him educationally.

Note: According to federal law, public school districts are required to provide a FAPE to every student with a handicap that lives within the school's jurisdiction, regardless of the severity of the handicap. If your child does not need an IEP, then the school district must make other accommodations through supplementary aids and services. A school must provide education for a handicapped child in the same setting as children who are not handicapped to the maximum extent appropriate. A school must therefore place your child in a regular educational environment unless the school demonstrates that education in the regular environment with the use of supplementary aids and services cannot be achieved satisfactorily. This includes the academic setting, as well as nonacademic and extracurricular services and activities.

Thought Question:

1. Assistive technology devices are various types of technology that could assist your child in learning, and they are becoming more popular. Do you have an assistive technology device you would like your child to use in school? If so, what device(s) are you seeking to use? How would it impact/improve your child's education?

_____
_____
_____
_____
_____

CASE EXAMPLE
(Residency)

H.P. v. Naperville Community Unit School District

H.P. attended the Naperville Central High School, which is part of the Naperville Community Unit, a school district in Illinois. She attended this school in her freshman, sophomore, and junior years. During her junior year, H.P.'s mother committed suicide, and her father moved with her outside of the school district. H.P., nonetheless, completed her junior year at the high school because the school district did not learn of her change in residency until just before the next school year. Under the school district's residency policy, "a student must establish residency within the School District boundaries in order to attend a School District School."

H.P.'s father asked the school district to waive its residency requirement to allow her to attend the same high school in her senior year as an accommodation for certain claimed disabilities under Title II of the ADA and Section 504 of the Rehabilitation Act of 1973, including anxiety, depression, sleep disturbances, and seizures. He was denied the request.

The father then filed a federal suit for disparate impact and disparate treatment under Title II and Section 504. The issue before the court was: Did the school district violate Title II or Section 504 when it prohibited H.P., a student with disabilities, from returning to the high school when she moved out of the district? The court found that no violations had occurred because it recognized that the school district disallowed H.P. from attending Naperville Central High School due to its residency policy, not because of her alleged disability. Additionally, the residency policy on its face treated identical nonresidents the same; thus, the only reason H.P. could not attend the high school was because she resided outside the district, which was unrelated to her disability.

CASE EXAMPLE
(Sports and Behavioral Disability)

Brown v. Elk Grove Unified School District

Isaiah Brown, a recent high school graduate, was a student with the disability of emotional disturbance. He had previously played on the high school's traveling basketball team, and was praised as one of the school's best junior varsity (JV) players. Nevertheless, he was the only JV player not invited to the school's summer basketball program, an unofficial prerequisite to joining the varsity team. Soon after, the varsity coach denied him a spot on the team's roster, claiming it was because he lacked defensive awareness. However, Brown alleges the real reason was because the coach had told other people he was "not going to deal" with Brown since "all he does is get upset" and "emotional." Brown's volatility derives from his emotional disturbance disability, for which he received special education services under an IEP. Brown transferred to two other schools in the hopes of playing basketball, but was denied the varsity team at each school because of the belief he was too emotional. The multiple school transfers and rejections affected his academic performance and emotional health. An academic scholarship to play college basketball in Wyoming was rescinded due to his lack of varsity experience, and he had to attend a different college without a basketball scholarship and as a "red-shirt freshman." The issue before the federal court: Did the school district violate Title II and Section 504 when it knew a child with emotional disturbance was being denied the ability to play on a varsity basketball team because of his emotional outbursts yet did nothing to address the issue? The court found that the school district had violated its duties. The case was analyzed under federal statutes, which are interpreted to read that, to establish a disability discrimination claim under Title II or under Section 504, a plaintiff must allege (1) a qualifying disability; (2) entitlement to participate in a public entity's services, program, or activities; and (3) exclusion from such services, programs, or activities based partially or solely on the disability. Because Brown sought damages, he had to allege that the district showed deliberate indifference, which, in this case, meant the school district both knew that a harm to a federally protected right was substantially likely and failed to act upon that likelihood.

When a school is on notice of needed accommodations, it is required to undertake a fact-specific investigation to determine what constitutes reasonable accommodation. A plaintiff may pursue a violation of Section 504 that denied meaningful access to a public benefit, which is what Brown did. In this case, at an early stage in the proceedings, the school district sought a dismissal before having to do an investigation into the allegations. The court ruled that when it came to causation, the complaint plausibly alleged that Brown's disability drove the exclusion, not his abilities as a player. He was the only JV player not promoted to varsity, and the only consistent summer league player not allowed to play the final summer that would have promoted him to varsity. Even when faced with too few players, the varsity coach promoted JV players rather than select Brown for the team. The other varsity coaches based their exclusion on his emotional state, at least in part, which directly links his emotional state to his disability. This is what helped prompt the court to rule that the parents sufficiently alleged the school district acted with deliberate indifference. The district knew about Brown's behavioral issues, and it knew he was denied a varsity spot because of his behavior. From this, it could be inferred that the district also noticed his decline in academic performance and well-being. Brown alleged the school district knew about his behavioral issues, knew how central basketball was to his life, and knew the three varsity coaches cited his emotional instability for not selecting him. However, his emotional instability is a manifestation of his emotional disability. Because the school district neither investigated the issue nor attempted to make accommodations after Brown complained, the court found meaningful access had been denied.

CASE EXAMPLE
(Allergy to Dogs and IEP)

Doe v. US Secretary of Transportation

Jane Doe had been diagnosed with a disability of chronic asthma and food and environmental allergies, including an allergy to dogs in which her asthma is triggered by dog dander and a protein emitted by dogs. Symptoms upon contact with dogs can include asthma attacks, hives, excessively runny or clogged nose, watery eyes, coughing, sneezing, nose bleeds, difficulty concentrating or performing the functions of daily living, and difficulty interacting with others. Dog dander and protein remain in an indoor space after the dog is removed, and even over time they do not necessarily lose their toxicity for people with allergies and asthma. Jane was in the sixth grade when she began experiencing increased asthma and allergy symptoms, requiring her parents to administer more medicine than usual. Her parents repeatedly asked the school to exclude dogs from the school property, but the school explained it could not comply as it was bound by federal and state laws to allow dogs. In mid-November 2014, however, the school invited the CEO of an organization that trains and promotes the use of service dogs to give a lecture to the sixth-grade students, and a service dog was brought as an example. In January 2015, Jane's parents requested that the school create an accommodation plan pursuant to Section 504 of the Rehabilitation Act of 1973. The plan required the district to prevent contact between Jane and service dogs, employ a cleaning protocol anywhere a service dog had been, and notify the parents of expected visits to school by a service dog. In May 2015, the school held a fundraiser for the service organization, and Jane's parents allege they were not notified of the event until a week before. In September 2015, the school district told Jane to sit in an auditorium near where the service dog had been the previous June, and she suffered asthma and allergy symptoms the following day. In November 2015, her class was planning a field trip to a nursing home where dogs regularly visited. The district proposed to keep the students in an area where dogs were not allowed and have Jane enter and exit through a different entrance than the other students. Jane ended up not going on the field trip, instead writing an essay. Jane's parents filed a complaint alleging the district was in violation of Section 504.

The issue before the court: Did the school district fail to make effective accommodations for Jane when she was confronted with other people who needed service animals? The court decided it had. It acknowledged that the school district's current 504 plan to accommodate Jane's disability required, among other things, that any service dog be kept thirty feet away; and the two previous 504 plans similarly required the district personnel to prevent contact between Jane and dogs. The court, however, also pointed out that the plans afforded Jane a reasonable accommodation under Title II and Section 504. The district was not free to ban all dogs from Jane's school, and she was not entitled to the accommodations she preferred. The court noted, though, that while public entities are not required to enact perfect accommodations for people with disabilities, the accommodations must be effective.

CASE EXAMPLE
(Sexual Assault Allegations)

Swanger v. Warrior Run School District

B.J.S. was a mentally challenged student in a special education and life skills program. M. was also a student in the special education and life skills program, and under the care of the county through foster care services. M. was also part of a nonprofit psychiatric treatment program called Diversified Treatment Alternatives (DTA) that provided counseling to PTSD individuals. M. had been accused of asking to touch a female student's breasts; an investigation was conducted and the school concluded he had not done that, and it implemented no preventative measures. Less than two months later, though, he was removed from the school and placed in alternative education after he had sexual contact with a chicken at his foster home. He was allowed to reenroll in B.J.S.'s school the following school year.

Shortly after re-enrollment, M. began talking to a male peer about a girl, and made a comment about touching her breasts. Again, no preventative measures were taken by the school, and he was seated directly behind B.J.S. in English class. He then was accused of touching her private areas. According to M., he asked B.J.S. if he could put his hand up her shirt and feel her breasts, and she nodded her head. He then asked if he could put his finger in her vagina, and she again nodded her head. He admitted to doing this two or three times in English class. When this was finally reported by a teacher to the school officials (it is not clear from the court records how the teacher learned about it), M. was removed from the school again.

Criminal charges were filed in which M. pleaded guilty to indecent assault. DTA had never shared any information regarding his sexual history, treatment notes, plans, or records with the school district. DTA also never discussed with the school district his care, treatment, and psychiatric/sexual history. B.J.S.'s parents sued the school district for, among other things, violations of Title II of the ADA and Section 504 of Rehabilitation Act. The issue before the court: Had the school district violated Section 504 when a student with sexual propensities sexually assaulted B.J.S., a fellow disabled student? In this case, the judge found the school district had not violated Section 504. The court said that B.J.S.'s parents failed to point to any causal relationship between their daughter's disability and misconduct toward her or show that her disability affected the decisions of the school district. Additionally, even assuming that school staff did know about M.'s sexual misconduct history or his sexual propensities, the parents had failed to demonstrate how this knowledge in and of itself led to discrimination based on B.J.S.'s disability.

There was no evidence that M. was not permitted to sit next to female students in his "regular" classes or that the school took extra precautions to protect students in regular classes but not students in special education classes. Similarly, there was no evidence that M. touched any other student in his special education classes or that any of the teachers or administrators were aware of his sexual advances toward B.J.S. or any other student in special education classrooms. For these reasons, the court ruled there was no evidence that the school district discriminated against female students in special education classes in any way. There was no evidence that the school district took any actions based on special education students' disabilities that rendered them more vulnerable to M.'s potential sexual misconduct, and there was no evidence to suggest that B.J.S. was treated differently than any other student, whether disabled or not.

> **Note**: The common thread in all of these cases is that the court was required to focus on a major issue, causation. The following are questions to think about if you believe your child is being discriminated against or treated differently.

Thought Questions:

1. Is your child being treated differently because of his or her disability? If so, how is this manifesting?

_____

_____

_____

_____

_____

2. Is your child being treated differently than nondisabled children? If so, how?

_____

_____

_____

_____

_____

3. If you believe your child has been treated differently, have you notified the school administration of this different treatment? If so, was it by phone call, email, or in person? When did you contact the school? What was the response? Who responded?

_____

_____

_____

_____

_____

Here is more information about 504 Service Agreements, but what follows is related to what happens if a school refers your child for aid, benefits, or services not provided by the school itself. In that case, the school must ensure that adequate transportation to and from the aid, benefits, or services is provided at no greater cost than would be incurred by you had your child received those same services by the school. If a public or private residential placement is deemed necessary, the placement, including nonmedical care and room and board, must be provided at no cost to you or your child. Disagreements regarding whether a school has made a FAPE available or other questions regarding who is financially responsible for the costs of a private school are subject to due process procedures. If a public school has made available a FAPE but you as a parent voluntarily decide to place your child in a private school, the public school is not required to pay for that education. If your decision to place your child in a private school was because you disagreed with the FAPE being offered, you can request a due process hearing, which is discussed in Step Four. If the hearing officer agrees with the school, however, you will not be entitled to tuition reimbursement. If the hearing officer agrees with you, then you could seek reimbursement.

If the public school places your child in a setting other than a regular educational environment, the school must take into consideration the proximity of that placement to your home. When interpreting evaluation data and making placement decisions, a school must consider information from a variety of sources, including aptitude and achievement tests, teacher recommendations, physical condition, social and cultural backgrounds, and adaptive behavior. The school must also establish procedures to ensure that (1) information obtained from all such sources is documented and carefully considered; (2) the placement decision is made by people knowledgeable about your child, the meaning of the evaluation data, and the placement options; and (3) the placement decision is made in conformity with the law.

CASE EXAMPLE
(Use of Body Sock)

Crochran v. Columbus City School

Crochran was a student diagnosed with autism and ADHD. One day he was acting out in class and his teacher tried to correct his behavior, but to no avail. At the suggestion of another teacher, Crochran's teacher asked him whether he wanted to use a body sock, which is a stretchy suit that is a therapeutic tool for children with autism. When he stepped into the suit, he fell down and injured his front teeth, requiring endodontic work. Crochran's parents brought a lawsuit asserting violations of Title II of the ADA and Section 504 of the Rehabilitation Act.

The issue before the court: Had the teacher violated Crochran's constitutional or statutory rights by using a body sock when other methods of behavior intervention had not worked? The court decided the teacher did not violate any rights. The court first considered the claim of a constitutional violation of the Fourth Amendment against unreasonable seizures. To qualify as a seizure in the school context, the limitation on the student's freedom of movement must significantly exceed that inherent in the everyday context. A seizure is permissible in its scope when the measures adopted are reasonably related to the objectives of the seizure and not excessive in light of the age and sex of the student and the nature of the infraction. Crochran had been acting out, and other methods of behavior correction had not worked. The teacher had seen body socks used with autistic children before and reasonably believed the sock could help. The teacher did not force Crochran to step inside it. Although the use of the body sock may have been negligent, Cochran's parents had not pointed to any evidence that the teacher's use of the body sock was not justified in a constitutional sense. Its use was reasonably related to the object of the seizure: calming Crochran down and trying to help him control his behavior. This was not excessive given the circumstances.

When looking at the Fourteenth Amendment (substantive due process), the court pointed out that the Due Process clause protects individuals from the arbitrary actions of government employees, but only the most egregious official conduct can be said to be arbitrary in the constitutional sense. The question the court had to answer was: Had the force applied caused injury so severe and was so disproportionate to the need presented, and was it inspired by malice or sadism rather than a merely careless or unwise excess of zeal, that it amounted to a brutal and inhumane abuse of official power. In this case, again, the teacher's actions may have been negligent, but they did not give rise to the statutory violations that the parents claimed. A legitimate pedagogical reason justified the teacher's use of the body sock, and the IEP described him as an autistic student who required a heavy work sensory warm-up or a reward system to be successful with fine motor or visual motor tasks. Body socks are used to help autistic students with sensory needs. Additionally, the teacher did not force him to get into the body sock. Although there was a serious injury, the other two factors were not met, which compelled the court to find that the teacher's actions were not egregious.

CASE EXAMPLE
(Use of Rifton Chair)

C.D. v. Arab City Board of Education

C.D. was a child who was eligible for special education and related services because he was developmentally delayed. C.D. attended a primary school beginning in kindergarten in the 2015–16 school year. From October 2015 to March 2016, C.D.'s teachers and staff documented disciplinary problems, such as hitting, punching, kicking, head-butting, pulling hair, and spitting at teachers and students; throwing rocks and chairs; rolling on the ground; screaming; and on one occasion exposing himself. One teacher testified that she had C.D. sit in a child-sized Rifton chair for a two-minute timeout when he was misbehaving. A Rifton chair is a wooden adaptive chair meant to be used by people with certain physical disabilities; it has a cloth strap with a three-prong buckle at the waist. C.D.'s grandmother, his guardian, took issue with use of the chair and wrote a letter to the school administration stating "she did not want C.D. to have access to or be placed in the Rifton chair for any reason." As a result, the school removed the chair from C.D.'s special education classroom and instructed its teachers that the Rifton chair, and any such chairs such as orthopedic medical transport chairs, could under no circumstances be used to address behavioral issues. C.D. was eventually moved to a self-contained special education classroom per agreement between the school and his grandmother.

On March 30, 2016, C.D. misbehaved at recess by hitting another child and throwing rocks in the air. As a result, a teacher transported C.D. to the front office using a transport restraint, which is described as involving physical support by a trained individual to a child's shoulders and elbows so as to prevent injury while the child is being escorted to another location. After the event, C.D. was removed from the school and the grandmother began homeschooling.

She filed a request for a due process hearing. The question before the hearing officer was: Had the school violated C.D.'s rights under Title II of the ADA and Section 504 of the Rehabilitation Act when they used restraints to control his behavior? The hearing official said the school had not violated either, and pointed out that the grandmother had presented no evidence of intentional discrimination or deliberate indifference. To the contrary, the evidence showed that after the grandmother (and C.D.'s father) complained, a school administrator had undertaken an investigation into the allegations and sent them a report with the findings.

Step Four

How Do You File a Complaint?

If you've read the first three steps and are still frustrated with your child's school and are not satisfied with testing results or carry-through, the next step would be to file a complaint. A complaint could be filed alleging, for example, that the school district violated matters including Child Find in Step One. You may be dissatisfied with your child's evaluation, educational placement, or implementation of the IEP or 504 Service Agreement, and feel your child has been denied a FAPE. The written complaint must be filed within two years of the *last known* incident being alleged, but it can include incidents or harm that occurred for more than two years. When filing a complaint, certain content must be included: the name of your child and the home address, the name of the school, a description of the problem, and a proposed solution. If your child is homeless, you must still provide a contact address.

The IDEA requires school districts to have procedures in place for parents and schools to resolve disputes. Check with your local district to determine to which state educational agency you would file a complaint. Once the complaint is filed with the agency, a copy will be sent to the Special Education director and/or superintendent of your local district.

In the description, be sure to include all the facts pertaining to the problem(s) your child faces, including educational, emotional, behavioral, and medical issues. Also include any and all changes proposed or considered by the school and any of your proposed changes refused by the school. Outline other possible solutions to the extent they are known and available.

After the school district receives the complaint, it has fifteen days to notify a hearing officer and the complaining party (i.e., you or your attorney) in writing if the complaint is insufficient. A complaint could be considered insufficient if any of the above-mentioned information is not included. Ultimately, though, it will be the hearing officer who decides whether a complaint is sufficient.

Within ten days, the school district must also respond to the parent (or the parent's lawyer, if one has been retained) with information as to why the district either proposed or refused to take the action raised in the complaint, and to explain other options the IEP team considered and why those options were rejected. The school district must include information describing each evaluation procedure, assessment, record, or report that it used as the basis for its proposed or refused actions. The district must also describe other factors it considered relevant to its proposed or refused actions, and must respond to any other allegations made within the complaint.

The district must also give the parent information about any free or low-cost legal services available to them in the area. Even before a due process complaint is filed, if a parent even *requests* free or low-cost legal or other advocacy services, the district is required to provide that information.

The rules of law that govern the complaint-filing process include federal statutes that also provide what is called a fee-shifting provision. This provision entitles the "prevailing party"—that is, whom the court finds for—reimbursement of attorney fees. This is true for both a case heard by a hearing officer in a due process hearing or a judge in a federal lawsuit. This provision can be enforced regardless of whether the prevailing party is the parent or school district. In this book, the terms "hearing officer" and "impartial hearing officer" are used interchangeably.

Damages awarded based on any *violation of the IDEA* and are meant to address educational harm. As a result, compensation comes in the form of additional education hours to make up for the lost school hours that lead to the educational harm. This is also known as compensatory education. Monetary damages are not awarded to redress educational harm. However, compensatory education can include tuition reimbursement costs paid to a private school if it was determined that private school placement was appropriate because of the public school's denial of a FAPE.

Damages awarded based on any *violation of Title II of the ADA or Section 504 of the Rehabilitation Act of 1973* are financial. In order to receive such payments, the party making the allegation must show deliberate indifference, as discussed in some Section Three case examples.

Alternatives to filing a due process complaint include a mediation or a facilitated meeting. Mediation is when the parties get together with a neutral mediator specially trained in special education law and conflict resolution. This mediator is provided by the administrative agency, and the mediator will help the parties try to negotiate a settlement. Mediation is non-adversarial and an alternative to a due process hearing; however, a mediation will not affect your rights to still have a due process hearing if a settlement can not be made. A facilitated meeting is when a neutral party, well-versed in special education law, attends an IEP meeting, with the goal of encouraging communication between the parties. The facilitator is provided by the administrative agency and the facilitator's role is to facilitate communication. As a result, the facilitator does not advocate on either party's behalf or play a role on either party's side. The facilitator is simply there to facilitate communication and assist with drafting the IEP to each party's satisfaction. Both of these alternatives come free of charge to parents.

CASE EXAMPLE
(Reimbursement of Attorney Fees)

R.C. v. Colonial School District[7]

A.D. attended public school in the Colonial School District until she was pulled out in the seventh grade by her mother, R.C., who thought the school had failed to provide her daughter with a FAPE, and instead enrolled A.D. in a private school. R.C. was now seeking tuition reimbursement and filed a due process complaint. A hearing officer found that A.D.'s IEP at Colonial School District was inappropriate, and that the placement at the private school was appropriate. The hearing officer awarded R.C. two years of compensatory education, tuition reimbursement for the current school year, and ongoing tuition reimbursement until the public school convened a meeting and wrote an appropriate IEP.

The following year, R.C. enrolled A.D. in the same private school for eighth grade, and the public school did not convene an

---

7 I don't include a lot of specific details about education and placement in this case because I want to focus on the reimbursement of attorney fees and when they are allowed. Attorneys may represent parents for free upfront because the statute allows for payment of attorney fees.

IEP meeting until the end of eighth grade for the following school year. R.C. again disputed the adequacy of the IEP and this time requested mediation. (A mediator is a neutral person chosen by the agency that received the complaint.) At the end of that summer (that is, just before ninth grade), R.C. notified Colonial School District she intended to enroll A.D. at a different private school for ninth grade, and requested reimbursement for tuition and related expenses. The school district responded that the new IEP placing A.D. at the public school in ninth grade was adequate. The mother cancelled the mediation and instead filed an administrative complaint challenging the adequacy of the IEP.

R.C. received a new IEP, in which the school district changed its offer and agreed to pay for private school tuition and transportation to the new private school. R.C. had ten days to respond, but did not do so for over a month, claiming that it did not constitute a valid offer because it lacked school board approval and failed to address her attorney's fees while waiting for the administrative hearing.

Both parties attended this administrative hearing, and the hearing officer again found in favor of R.C., ordering private school placement for A.D. The significance of this ruling is that it now made R.C. the prevailing party. Even though the hearing officer gave R.C. a ruling to which the district had already agreed, the district was silent on the issue of paying attorney fees. As the prevailing party, the mother then filed a claim in district court for reimbursement of all of her attorney fees related to the latest IEP.

The issue before the district court was: Had the public school district limited R.C.'s eligibility to be reimbursed for attorney fees with its ten-day settlement offer by not including wording about these expenses? The court ruled that a parent is substantially justified in rejecting an offer that does not include the (re)payment of attorney's fees only when the school district can reasonably expect that attorney's fees have accrued.[8] Generally, the IDEA provides for attorney's fees so that parents may seek assistance when necessary to protect their child's right to a FAPE. Up until this case, however, there was no controlling case law regarding whether or not the absence of wording regarding reimbursement of attorney's fees provided substantial justification for outright rejection of a settlement offer. The district court acknowledged that

---

8 Some attorneys require their clients to pay upfront and then seek reimbursement if they win in court. When parents seek reimbursement, it's actually to recover the money they paid the lawyer upfront.

the IDEA did not require a school district to include attorney fees in ten-day offers to parents. To be reimbursed for attorney fees, parents must be the prevailing (i.e., winning) party in court with a judgment on the main legal issue(s). The district court decided that the IDEA did not force parents to decide between the resolution of a placement dispute and paying for the attorney who assisted in achieving an appropriate placement for the student. However, the district court awarded R.C. reimbursement of her attorney's fees only for work performed prior to the ten-day offer, but held that because she did not receive more favorable relief and was not substantially justified in rejecting the ten-day offer, she was not entitled to lawyer fees accrued after the ten-day offer and while waiting for the administrative hearing to occur.

The court recognized that had R.C. accepted the ten-day offer, the parties—meaning the school district and R.C.—would have created a non-judicially sanctioned agreement—that is, neither party would be considered the prevailing party and R.C. would not be able to recover attorney fees. Because she hadn't accepted the offer, then her attorney fees were relevant but only for the work done up to the 10-day offer because the IEP had agreed to private school placement.

Note: The IDEA offers a provision for attorney's fees for parents seeking to protect their child's right to a FAPE, but the district court in this case acknowledged the IDEA does not require a school district to include attorney fees in its ten-day offer letters.

In my opinion, as the writer of this book, a school district seeking to settle a dispute in which a lawyer has been previously involved should acknowledge that the parent has accrued attorney's fees and should clearly state in its offer letter whether or not it includes the payment of such fees.

CASE EXAMPLE

Lincoln-Sudbury Regional School District v. W.W.

W.W. was a minor child who attended Lincoln-Sudbury High School. Early in the school year, on September 30, 2012, she was injured during a field hockey practice and suffered a concussion, causing her to miss school. Her medical doctor's orders were communicated to the school, which complied with them in all respects when she returned to school. Various accommodations were made to help W.W. catch up on the work she missed. Nevertheless, W.W. struggled in her intensive math class throughout the school year. Eight months after the concussion, her math teacher recommended that W.W. take an advanced but less rigorous course the following year. Her parents then claimed that W.W. was disabled, and that the school failed to provide reasonable accommodations. In September 2013, the parents removed W.W. from the public high school and enrolled her at a private school, and then brought a proceeding before the state's Board of Special Education Appeals.

The question before the hearing officer: Had W.W. been denied access to the school curriculum because reasonable accommodations weren't provided? The hearing officer found in favor of the school district: W.W. was not denied access. The hearing officer also found that the parents' claim was "patently frivolous" and filed for an "improper purpose." The school district then filed a lawsuit in district court to recover its attorneys' fees and costs. It sought $200,412.50 in attorneys' fees plus $5,167.61 in related costs and expenses.

The district court agreed with the hearing officer's finding that the parents' claims were frivolous, and found that an award of reasonable fees was proper. In the end, an appellate court, to which the court case had moved, reduced the fees but still required the parents to pay the school district $188,996.15 in fees and $2,052.21 in costs.

> **Note**: Fee reimbursement can work in the favor of the parents or the school. Courts that rule in a school district's favor will require the parents to pay the school district's legal fees. Requesting reimbursement from the parents is not the norm, and many districts don't request such reimbursement even if they win, but it is possible. As in W.W.'s case, the fees can be staggering and come as a terrible blow to the parents.

CASE EXAMPLE

L.H. v. Hamilton County Department of Education

L.H. had been diagnosed with Down Syndrome. From 2009–13 (kindergarten to second grade) he attended Normal Park Elementary School, a public school. In May 2013, his parents rejected the latest IEP for third grade and instead enrolled him in a Montessori school for the 2013–14 school year. L.H. continued to attend that school from third through eighth grades. His parents paid the costs of his private education and also paid for a full-time aide to assist L.H., although the Montessori school had an aide on staff.

After years of paying for private school placement, the parents filed a complaint alleging a denial of a FAPE in 2017. The district court found for the parents in that placement based on the 2013 IEP was more restrictive than necessary and therefore improper. The court, however, also determined that L.H.'s alternative private placement at the Montessori school did not satisfy the IDEA (the court transcript did not go in detail on this), so L.H.'s parents were not entitled to reimbursement. Both parties appealed to the US Court of Appeals for the 6th Circuit.

The appellate court's question was: What can be included in reimbursement costs? The 6th Circuit Court agreed that the public school's 2013 IEP was too restrictive but disagreed that the Montessori school did not satisfy the IDEA, and thus L.H.'s parents were entitled to reimbursement. The circuit court decided these reimbursement costs can include the same costs and fees that L.H.'s parents would have occurred had the district not violated the IDEA. In this case, the court looked at all the evidence presented and found that a total of $103,274 for L.H.'s full tuition and full-time private aide to be the appropriate amount of reimbursement. However, the court did not award reimbursement for costs for items purchased through L.H.'s pay card because the costs of school lunches, school supplies, and other miscellaneous items would have been borne by L.H.'s parents even if L.H. continued in public education.

CASE EXAMPLE
(Monetary Damages after-the-fact)

Somberg v. Utica Community Schools

Dylan was twenty-four at the time of this case. He had been diagnosed with autism, ADHD, Tourette syndrome, and Obsessive-Compulsive Disorder (OCD). During the 2012–13 school year, he was eighteen years old and in his fifth year of high school. His IEP had annual goals and provided that his IEP team would implement and document a trial of assistive technology: he would receive a 50/50 curriculum between special education and general education classes. The school district also attempted to place him in community-based inclusion (CBI) for the last two periods of his school day, but that was inconsistent with his IEP. After his parents objected to CBI, the district provided instruction in the principal's office for the last two periods. However, his parents then felt that Dylan was being secluded from other students and thus not receiving homework or other meaningful benefit.[9] His parents withdrew him from the district and enrolled him in a private school, and filed a due process complaint al-

---

9 For more on this term, see the section titled "Post the Endrew F. Case" at the end of this book.

leging the newest IEP did not provide Dylan with a FAPE. The hearing officer's findings were a mixed bag.

The officer found for the parents in that their son had been denied a FAPE because only one of the IEP goals was measurable as required by the IDEA and because the transition plan was woefully inadequate.[10] However, the hearing officer found for the school district saying it had not violated any procedural requirements in developing the IEP, and that the parents had not established that their son's IEP was inconsistent with the IDEA's least restrictive environment requirement. The parents appealed the hearing officer's finding that the school district had complied with procedural requirements and that it had failed to award compensatory education.

The district court's question was: Were the parents entitled to backward-looking relief in the form of compensatory education for their son? Recognizing that compensatory education is designed to remedy past educational failings, the district court ruled for the parents. In coming to this conclusion, the court noted that an award of compensatory education would provide meaningful relief to Dylan as a remedy for the district's past IDEA violations. The fact that he was not currently a student in the school district's system was irrelevant because the relief would reimburse the family for the cost of obtaining educational services that ought to have been provided free with a correct IEP.

On appeal to the 6th Circuit, the school district argued that the district court had improperly ordered it to pay for twelve hundred hours of tutoring and one year of transition planning, as opposed to ordering it to provide those services to Dylan. The appellate court recognized that the Supreme Court precedent was that monetary damages were not appropriate to remedy violations of the IDEA; however, this circuit court concluded it could award judgment for what it would now cost Dylan to obtain the educational services he ought to have received earlier, and that type of an award would not constitute damages.

---

10 A transition plan in an IEP outlines how a student will transition from one school to the next, such as from middle school to high school, and even from high school to the real world after graduation.

Exhaustion

The Importance of Doing Things in the Right Order

A major legal hurdle is the issue of what is known as exhaustion. Generally speaking, a party must exhaust administrative remedies through a due process hearing in front of a hearing officer before filing a complaint to be heard in a federal district court before a judge. If a party has not fully exhausted the remedies through an administrative process, then a federal court will dismiss the case for lack of jurisdiction and require the party to refile appropriately at the administrative level. After a decision is made by a hearing officer, parents may seek a review of that decision by a State Review Officer. In some states, a review by the SRO is required; however, in other states, a party can appeal a hearing officer's decision directly to federal court. Check with your state's requirements to determine whether a SRO must review the decision before appealing to a federal court.

CASE EXAMPLE
Doucette v. Jacobs[11]

B.D. was diagnosed with Isodicentric Chromosome 15q Duplication Syndrome, a rare genetic disorder. As a result of this syndrome, B.D. has a number of substantial educational limitations, including global developmental delay, with a diagnosis of Pervasive Developmental Disability, Not Otherwise Specified, autism, seizure disorder, anxiety disorder, sleep disorder, and gastrointestinal issues. Children with this particular syndrome have an increased risk of sudden unexpected death caused by respiratory or cardiac arrest. B.D.'s parents contend that this

---

[11] Jacobs was a school staff member personally named in the lawsuit, rather than the school district.

increased risk is typically correlated with seizure activity; thus, the prevention of seizures is of critical importance.

B.D. was attending Perley Elementary School, where he received special education and related services. He attended school during the regular school year and over the summer as a part of an extended school year. His parents were not satisfied with the services their son was receiving in the school district, but they kept him there from age three until age six. His parents allege he suffered physical and emotional harm, including five stress-induced life-threatening tonic-clonic seizures (what used to be called grand mal seizures), due to the district's failure to provide him with appropriate services in school. In these types of seizures, among many other symptoms, a person's body stiffens and they may lose consciousness or bite their own tongue; their body will jerk rapidly; they could lose bladder or bowel control and have difficulty breathing.

After these seizures, B.D.'s parents requested that his IEP be amended to include a seizure plan; however, personnel were never properly trained, so the plan was not followed. The parents continued to complain verbally and in emails to the school district about B.D.'s safety and well-being. They complained:

> *[The school] was not implementing the kinds of interventions he needed to learn, that his aides were not appropriately trained, that he was not receiving sufficient sensory therapies, that he was not being monitored closely and was bolting from class, that he was becoming more aggressive toward other students, and that, after falling and hitting his head, his medical condition and disability were not taken into consideration and he was not provided proper care.*

His parents subsequently removed him from Perley Elementary School, and the seizures allegedly stopped. They filed a Request for Hearing with the Massachusetts Bureau of Special Education Appeals seeking an out-of-school-district placement for B.D. for the 2010–11 school year on the basis that the proposed IEP was inappropriate. They also sought compensatory services for the class time B.D. missed after seizures occurred at the school.

The hearing officer found for the school district, stating that the school district was an appropriate placement because it could amend B.D.'s IEP through additions and modifications, and because it had the capacity to develop an appropriate Applied Behavior Analysis based substantially in a separate classroom placement for B.D. at the start of the 2010–11 school year. The parents had no choice but to send B.D. to Perley in September 2010. However, B.D.'s seizure activity increased after he returned to school, and the parents allege that despite assurances from the school, it was not prepared to handle his seizure activity correctly. As a result, their son was again sent home on several occasions, which caused him to lose additional educational and developmental opportunities and to suffer a disruption in his schedules and routines. B.D. then received a service dog specially trained and certified to provide autism assistance service and assist with behavior disruption, anxiety, balance, and seizure alerting. B.D. was not permitted to bring his service dog to school. After experiencing another seizure while at summer school, the IEP committee finally agreed to place B.D. in an out-of-school-district placement.

The parents allege B.D. has made developmental and educational progress and has not suffered a seizure since being moved to a new school. His parents then filed a complaint in federal court. The issue for the court was: Had B.D.'s parents exhausted the administrative review process with respect to their claims under Section 504 of the Rehabilitation Act of 1973 before they could move forward with the current lawsuit?

The district court outlined that the U.S. Supreme Court in Napoleon v. Fry had found that exhaustion is not necessary when the the substance of a grievance is something other than the denial of the IDEA's core guarantee—that is, a FAPE. However, if a lawsuit charges a denial of a FAPE, the parents cannot bring a lawsuit under a statute other than the IDEA. In determining whether a suit seeks relief for denial of a FAPE, a court should look to the substance of the parents' complaint, not the labeling of the complaint. To determine the substance, the court needs to answer two questions: (1) Could the parents have brought essentially the same claim if the alleged conduct had occurred at a public facility that was not a school, such as a public theater or library? (2) Could an adult at the school, such as an employee or visitor, have pressed essentially the same grievance? If the answers to the two questions are yes, it is not a complaint that expressly alleges the denial of a FAPE, because in these other situations there is no FAPE obligation and yet the same suit could go forward. If one or both answers are no, then the complaint probably does concern a FAPE, even if it does not explicitly say so. Determining the substance of a suit in the denial of a FAPE can even emerge from the history of the proceedings; for example, a court may consider that parents previously invoked formal procedures related to the IDEA during a dispute, thus previously starting to exhaust the act's remedies.

In this case, the court found that the parents' entire complaint was based on (1) B.D.'s inadequate IEP; (2) a concern that he was not receiving appropriate services in his public education (and thus was being denied a FAPE); and (3) the lack of such services was causing B.D. serious harm. As further evidence that the parents' claims related to the denial of a FAPE, they had previously invoked IDEA's formal procedures.

Their claims relating to the denial of B.D.'s use of a service dog were part and parcel of their contentions about the failure of the district to provide a FAPE, and is the type of complaint that could appropriately be raised before the Bureau of Special Education Appeals in connection with a challenge to an IEP. The court thus ruled that the parents had not exhausted the administrative review process and could not move forward with their federal lawsuit. The parents' claim of a civil rights violation, under Title II of the ADA and Section 504, due to the school not allowing the use of the service dog in school was also dismissed since it too was related to a denial of a FAPE.

CASE EXAMPLE

S.D. v. Haddon Heights Board of Education

S.D., whose age wasn't revealed in the court case, suffers from multiple medical problems, including chronic sinusitis with frequent acute exacerbations, allergic rhinitis, and intermittent asthma. His doctor concluded that these medical problems make it likely that S.D. will have frequent school absences due to an acute underlying chronic illness, and suggested that he could qualify for accommodations under a 504 Service Agreement. The school district developed an accommodation plan that included providing extra time to complete assignments, tests, and quizzes. It required the parents to communicate with S.D.'s teachers about any missed work and absences. His parents allege that the initial 504 plan was not properly implemented or effective.

An amended 504 plan, dated April 19, 2013, required S.D.'s teachers to send weekly updates to the parents about S.D.'s missing assignments and to provide class notes about the lesson(s) he missed when he was absent. While it allowed teachers to reduce assignments at their discretion, it also required S.D. to complete his assignments within two weeks of any absence; to create a to-do list of homework; to keep folders of complete and incomplete work; and to communicate with teachers, the guidance counselor, and the school nurse about any issues relating to his school work or the inability to keep pace. Even though S.D. accrued thirty-three absences in the school year, most of which related to his disabilities, he passed his grade. In summer 2013, the school district enacted a new attendance policy for the 2013–14 school year that required students to be retained if they accrued more than thirty-three absences in a school year, regardless of whether the absences were "excused, approved, or unexcused." By March 2014, S.D. had accumulated thirty-seven absences due to his disability, all of which were excused by medical notes.

The school informed S.D.'s parents that their son would be left back pursuant to the new attendance policy. After receiving the principal's letter, the parents filed a complaint with the US Department of Education, Office for Civil Rights. However, they then filed a lawsuit in federal court, including a motion for a preliminary injunction seeking to stop the district from retaining their son based on the number of absences. The school district filed a motion to dismiss, arguing that the federal court did not have jurisdiction to hear the case.

The issue for the court was: Did the parents need to first exhaust administrative remedies for a school's attendance policy that posed educational harm to their child? Section 1415(l) of the IDEA requires exhaustion of the administrative hearing process not only in actions brought directly under the IDEA but also in non-IDEA actions where the parents seek relief under the IDEA. As explained in the previous case, this means that if a lawsuit is filed relating to the denial of a FAPE, a parent cannot bring a suit under any statute other than the IDEA. The court cited the factors outlined from the Napoleon v. Fry case mentioned previously.

The allegations in the complaint asserted: (1) S.D.'s discrimination claims, which arose from educational harm; (2) a challenge to the appropriateness of the school district's initial decision to retain S.D. in the tenth grade; (3) the school district's enactment of the revised attendance policy to retain students based on a total number of absences; and (4) the school district's choice of make-up courses to allow S.D. to progress to the eleventh grade. Based on those allegations, the court concluded that the parents' claims of discrimination and retaliation were subject to the IDEA's exhaustion requirement, and thus the parents had to go before an administrative agency first.

CASE EXAMPLE

Matthews v. Douglas County School District RE 1

J.U. was a student at Legend High School, and the parents challenged the district's provision of a FAPE. This case arose from a second due process complaint that included many of the same grievances as in the first due process complaint. The second complaint was also dismissed by the hearing office on procedural grounds: the parents had failed to participate in the resolution process required under federal law (34 C.F.R. Section 300.510). This section creates a process in which school districts, using reasonable efforts, must contact parents who have filed a due process complaint to engage in a resolution meeting where differences can be discussed in an effort to resolve the dispute. The resolution period is thirty days, and if the school district cannot obtain parents' participation in this timeframe, it may move to dismiss the complaint.

J.U.'s parents filed a third complaint, and the question before the court was: Had the hearing officer wrongly dismissed the second due process complaint? The final determination went again in favor of the school, and was based on the district's submission of sixteens exhibits detailing its efforts to schedule the resolution meeting with J.U.'s parents, and the parents' refusal to participate each time.

Note: I have included this case, using limited details as to the complaint, to show the significance of parent participation and cooperation. By the time a case gets to the point of litigation, it is very contentious and many times parents have no desire to even negotiate with the school. This case shows that the law requires parents to first seek a resolution. I've left out many of the details in order to highlight that a due process complaint case can be dismissed because parents refuse to attend a resolution meeting.

Bullying and Your Disabled Child

One consistent, ongoing issue in the education world is bullying, which is not expressly covered by the IDEA or Section 504 of the Rehabilitation Act. This issue is usually litigated under constitutional violations, or sometimes state law violations if you live in a state with an anti-bullying statute. The following cases are samples of how federal courts have addressed the issue as violations of the United States Constitution.

CASE EXAMPLE
T.C. v. Hempfield Area School District

T.C. was a high school student eligible for special education based on his disabilities of autism and other health impairments. In January 2014, T.C. was also diagnosed with Crohn's disease. At an IEP meeting in April 2014, the IEP team and T.C.'s parents agreed that T.C. would be enrolled the following school year in the Central Westmoreland Career and Technology Center, which he would begin the tenth grade. At this IEP meeting, T.C.'s parents expressed concerns about their son's safety, since he had informed them about the bullying he was currently experiencing. His father had already informed the high school special education teacher about the incidents, and the teacher had contacted the school district representative about them.

An IEP team meeting to address the reported bullying incidents was held in the new school year, on September 29, 2015. The team learned that at the Tech Center, T.C. had been physically assaulted by peers; was locked in a room; and could not use the bathroom because other students pounded on the restroom door when he was inside. The IEP team then revised T.C.'s IEP to allow him to return to the regular high school full-time. In April 2016, T.C. revealed in therapy he was sodomized with a broomstick by students at the Tech Center. The principal of the Tech Center initiated an investigation, which concluded that none of the incidents, as verified by the video surveillance footage, rose to the level of bullying according to school policy.

T.C.'s parents filed a due process complaint, and the hearing officer concluded that while bullying had occurred, the district was not deliberately indifferent because it hadn't violated its own bullying policy; thus, it had not violated Title II of the ADA or Section 504 of the Rehabilitation Act.

The parents appealed to a federal district court. The issue was whether the school had violated Title II rights through what is known as associational discrimination; that is, by not informing T.C.'s parents of the events occurring at the Tech Center. The court found the school was in violation. Under both Section 504 and Title II, nondisabled individuals have standing to bring claims when they are injured because of their association with a disabled person. To claim associational discrimination, a plaintiff (in this case, T.C.'s parents) must allege: (1) a logical and significant association with an individual with disabilities; (2) that a public entity (in this case, the school) knew of that association; (3) that the public entity discriminated against them because of that association; and (4) they suffered a direct injury as a result of the discrimination. An associational discrimination claim must be something more than a disagreement about the direction of a student's IEP and the provision of services.

The court first pointed out an IEP team meeting must include all members so they can offer suggestions and opinions that benefit the student. In this case, the parents alleged that the Tech Center staff had failed to provide them with significant information even after the staff learned about T.C.'s harassment. Because they weren't made aware, they could not engage in meaningful participation in IEP meetings, where they would have likely sought changes to the IEP to address the bullying. While not sharing the information with the parents about how T.C. was treated at the Tech Center certainly created a direct injury to T.C., it was also plausible that it deprived the parents of their right to meaningful participation in IEP team meetings.

CASE EXAMPLE

Bowe v. Eau Claire Area School District

C.B., whose age was not given in the court transcript, was diagnosed with Asperger's Syndrome, and was the victim of bullying in middle and high schools. Students called him gay, queer, fag, pussy, douche bag, and shit stain, and they put gum in his hair, threatened to kill his family, told him to "go fucking die," left a bag of feces at his house, and egged his house. C.B. and his parents complained of more than thirty discrete acts of bullying while C.B. attended these schools from 2008 until he graduated in 2015. The school district investigated each complaint, which generally involved interviewing the students involved and sometimes referring the matter to the police or speaking to the classroom teacher. If the investigation uncovered inappropriate action, the school district responded with calls to C.B.'s home or with corrective action plans.

These plans ranged from counseling the bullying student to that student's suspension, and in some cases referral for criminal charges. Even so, C.B.'s parents sued the school district and its principal and vice principal in federal district court alleging they were deliberately indifferent to the harassment and bullying that C.B. suffered as a student.

The issue before the court was: Had the school been deliberately indifferent even though staff responded to each instance of bullying through various forms of punishment or consequence, yet the bullying continued? The court found the school hadn't been deliberately indifferent, and noted the parents did not prove this in their claims. In this case, the school had investigated every instance of bullying that C.B. or his parents brought to its attention, and staff addressed confirmed acts of bullying with corrective action. The court found that the school had favored counseling over more severe types of discipline, but that appeared to have worked in at least in some instances, so the school was clearly not unreasonable for continuing to use it.

CASE EXAMPLE

Spring v. *Allegany-Limestone Central School District*

G.S. was a special education student who suffered from disabilities, including Tourette's syndrome, ADHD, and Callosum Dysgenesis (a brain malformation). He often experienced challenges with social interactions due to difficulty imagining potential consequences of behavior, being insensitive to the thoughts and feelings of others, and misunderstanding social cues. His parents alleged these disabilities impacted his ability to speak, learn, read, concentrate, think, and communicate. Tourette's presented in the form of motor and vocal tics, including regular and frequent swallowing sounds; outbursts; involuntary knee slapping, eye blinking, and compulsive cracking of his neck and wrists; repetitive utterance of foul language, including the "F" word; and repetitive questioning.

In April 2012, G.S. was disciplined and removed from the school's baseball team as a result of horseplay. In November 2012, G.S. physically responded to unrelenting harassment and bullying by a fellow student; he was immediately suspended, yet no manifestation determination hearing was conducted.[12] The parents alleged that the bullying G.S. endured was minimized, dismissed, or ignored by the school district's staff and its officials.

The court had to decide: Had the school showed deliberate indifference to disability-based bullying, and had it failed to take corrective action? The court found for the parents because there were numerous allegations of conduct consistent with disability-related harassment. These included allegations that G.S. was subjected to acts of fear and intimidation: teasing, taunting, bullying, name-calling, violence, offensive touching, hitting, interference with relationships, and public and private humiliation. The allegations included that the conduct was motivated in whole or part by his disabilities. The court noted that mimicry of a disability, together with mocking comments, had

---

[12] A manifestation determination hearing is conducted when a disabled child's conduct may warrant disciplinary action by the school for more than 10 consecutive school days. In a manifestation determination hearing, the IEP team will meet with the disabled child's parent(s) and talk to any witness(es) to the incident to determine whether the conduct was a manifestation of the student's disability. If it was, then no discipline action will be taken. If it was not, then the student could be disciplined in accordance with the school's code of conduct policies.

held in other cases when determining whether harassment was related to disability in an ADA hostile-work-environment. Similarly, insults that specially referenced the perceived nature of a plaintiff's disability have been found to support a disability discrimination claim. The court also found that the assistant principal took no action in response to the numerous complaints. He alleged that G.S. was "just trying to get his harassers in trouble," which may also be construed as an unreasonable response to the report of disability-related bullying. The remaining school officials, however, could not be considered to be deliberately indifferent because they either made no allegations they were aware of the bullying, or if they had noticed were unaware it was related to his disability.

Thought Questions:

1. Is your child getting bullied by other children in school because of his or her disability? If so, how is it manifesting? Be specific with names of students, the exact words used for name-calling and/or the actions used in bullying, and be as specific as possible about the date(s) this occurred.

_____

_____

_____

_____

2. If your child is getting bullied by other children at the school, you must place a school on notice of the conduct. Unfortunately, this can place your child at risk of continuing to be a victim, but a court cannot hold a school district responsible for conduct about which the school district did not know. Did you inform any school officials? If so, was it the teacher(s), the guidance counselor(s), the principal, the superintendent?

_____

_____

_____

_____

_____

3. When did you notify the school officials? How did you make this notification: in writing, via email, over the phone, or in person?

___

4. What was the school official's response? Remember, courts will consider whether the school responded appropriately, not whether its response matched your request. In the event of litigation, this information becomes relevant.

___

5. Were any children disciplined? If so, how?

___

The Endrew F. Case

How Courts Have Considered "Meaningful Benefit"

If you aren't familiar yet with the *Endrew F. v. Douglas County School District* court case, you soon will be. Everyone who has spent any time in the special education world knows of this US Supreme Court case. If you don't know or as a reminder if you do, Endrew was a student who made several requests to have a service animal with her in school, which the school denied each time. The Court held that the school had violated her rights under Title II of the ADA and Section 504 of the Rehabilitation Act. With this case, the Court overruled its previous longstanding position of *de minimus* (i.e., too minor to take under consideration) benefit by holding that a school is required to ensure a disabled child receives an education that is more than the minimum. Instead, a FAPE needs to provide meaningful benefit, and if it does not the school has violated the child's rights. Since this determination, courts around the country have wrestled with defining the phrase "meaningful benefit" and if a student has received an education that is more than *de minimus*.

CASE EXAMPLE

F.L. v. Board of Education of the Great Neck Union Free School District

R.C.L. was a child with various learning disabilities including: (1) attention deficit hyperactivity disorder ("ADHD"); (2) severe predominantly inattentive presentation; (3) developmental co-ordination disorder; (4) severe specific learning disorder with impairment in reading; (5) severe specific learning disorder with impairment in written expression; and (6) moderate to severe specific learning disorder with impairment in mathematics. In addition to his learning disabilities, R.C.L. also suffered from auditory processing disorder, apraxia, and severe oculomotor and visual processing delays. As a result of these disabilities, R.C.L. had significant difficulties with reading, mathematics, fine motor skills, pragmatic language, executive functioning, visual tracking, visual memory, auditory processing, attention, behavioral functioning, social functioning, and emotional functioning. The school district provided many accommodations but it wasn't until after R.C.L. scored a one (the lowest score) on several district-wide assessments that he was evaluated for and received and IEP. R.C.L.'s IEP provided for aids, including speech therapy, reading instruction in a special class setting, and occupational therapy. The IEP also provided corresponding goals for R.C.L. to achieve for supports such as OT and speech therapy. While he met some of his goals, he never achieved all of his goals. The school district continued to change R.C.L.'s IEP in an attempt to allow him to continue to work towards his goals.

His parents filed a due process complaint alleging that the school district denied R.C.L. a FAPE and the IEP was inadequate. They argued that three years' worth of IEPs denied their son a FAPE when the district did not extend school year services over the summer and did not provide the requested specific private reading services, causing R.C.L. to do poorly on tests. The hearing officer agreed a FAPE had been denied and ordered compensatory services and reimbursement. However, the school appealed, and at the next step the State Review Officer (SRO) disagreed and reversed the hearing officer's decision. The parents appealed again to a federal district court. The issue was: Had R.C.L. been denied a FAPE when he was not allowed to attend summer school or provided private reading services, and thus did not perform well on standardized tests? The court found he had not been denied a FAPE.

First, it is important to know that when a hearing officer and SRO disagree, a reviewing judge in federal court generally will defer to the SRO's final decision unless the judge determines that the decision was inadequately reasoned. If that is the case, then the judge may consider a better-reasoned opinion by the hearing officer.

In this instance, the district court agreed with the SRO's opinion that each year's IEP presented a description of R.C.L.'s strengths, challenges, and goals that were consistent with the information before the CSE at each of the IEP meetings. The district court noted that the SRO had acknowledged modifications made in response to changes in R.C.L.'s evaluations and requests from his parents. The SRO had appropriately determined that R.C.L.'s IEPs were reasonably calculated to provide some meaningful benefit. When R.C.L.'s father showed evidence that goals were repeated on the IEPs, and that R.C.L. did poorly on standardized tests, the SRO had examined the issues. The SRO determined that the weight of the evidence demonstrated R.C.L. was progressing, even if not at a pace his parents preferred. The court noted that the Supreme Court in Endrew F. emphasized the IDEA requires an educational program reasonably calculated to enable a child to make progress appropriate in light of the child's circumstances, but that an educational program does not need to include grade-level advancement if that kind of progress is not a reasonable prospect for that particular child. An educational program must be appropriately ambitious in light of a child's special circumstances, just as advancement from grade to grade is appropriately ambitious for most children in regular classrooms. The goals may differ per student, but every child should have the chance to meet challenging objectives.

CASE EXAMPLE
S.M. v. Arlotto[13]

S.M. attended Anne Arundel County Public Schools. During second grade, the district established an IEP that identified S.M. as having a primary disability of developmental delay, and his affected skill areas were fine motor, reading, math, written expression, and requisite learning. Under the school's tracking system, S.M. was at grade level for reading, math, written expression, and requisite learning skills, but the IEP noted he had difficulty completing tasks without verbal prompts and difficulty remaining focused in a large group setting. The IEP provided that S.M. would receive seven and one-half hours of special education services each week in a co-taught education setting for language arts, math, and requisite learning; instructional and testing accommodations with aids; and thirty minutes of occupational therapy two times each week.

There were at least five IEP team meetings while S.M. was in second grade, and a communication log was instituted between the school and the parents. In the spring, the parents had a private neuropsychological evaluation—that is, an IEE—conducted in which the doctor concluded that S.M. had relative weaknesses in executive functioning, phonological awareness, visual motor integration, and sustaining attention and effort. In June, the district and the parents met to review the IEP for necessary revisions. The parents were dissatisfied with the draft IEP for the upcoming third grade, which identified S.M. as having a primary disability of a specific learning disability, and his affected skills areas were again fine motor, reading, math, written expression, and requisite learning schools. Under the tracking system for each school subject matter, the IEP noted that S.M. was at grade level for sight words and comprehension in reading, but at a first-grade level for decoding. In math he was at grade level for numerical operations, but only midyear/end-of-first-grade levels for problem solving and math fluency. In written expression, S.M. was at midyear first-grade levels for alphabet writing fluency, sentence composition, and spelling. As for fine motor and requisite learning skills, S.M. was below

---

13 Arlotto was a named school representative who was personally sued.

expectations. The IEP for third grade noted that S.M.'s services would include:

- twenty hours of extended school year services during the summer;
- ten and one-half hours of special education services a week in a cotaught general education setting for language arts, math, and requisite learning;
- thirty minutes of self-contained, pull-out class services taught by a special education teacher;
- instructional and testing accommodations with aids; and
- thirty minutes of occupational therapy three times a week.

In August, the parents notified the district they rejected the IEP for third grade because it provided for S.M. to be taught in a general educational setting with twenty to twenty-five students, and did not believe the IEP sufficiently emphasized S.M.'s issues with attention, dyslexia, or work avoidance behaviors.

The parents enrolled their son at a private school for special education and requested reimbursement. Toward the end of third grade year, an attorney sent the school district a letter indicating S.M. had flourished during his year at a private school and requested a meeting to revise S.M.'s IEP for the fourth grade. The IEP team met with the parents and made revisions to the IEP, but the parents again expressed concerns about the size of the proposed classes at the public school. They decided to keep S.M. at the private school. This IEP process occurred again during the fourth and fifth grades, which is when the parents filed a due process complaint.

The question before the hearing officer: Had the school district denied S.M. a FAPE when he made better progress at a private school? The hearing officer found for the school district, holding that the parents had failed to prove their case. The parents appealed. The issue before the district court was the same, and the court again found for the school district, saying the IEPs and proposed placement at the public school were reasonably calculated to provide a FAPE for all school years. This court deferred to the hearing officer, with the additional conclusion that the US Supreme Court standard does not require the school district to provide a disabled child with the best possible education but only with meaningful benefit. A parent's insistence that a private school setting is more appropriate does not establish the inappropriateness of the public school, even if the child benefits more in the private setting. The parents' main argument was that S.M. required classes with a smaller teacher-student ratio, but the district court decided that the IEP team had constructed a schedule whereby S.M. would be provided instruction in self-contained classes, and would be with his nondisabled peers in a regular educational environment with the help of supplementary aids. Each IEP had ensured that S.M. received the attention and instruction he needed through a combination of co-taught, self-contained, and general education classes, while ensuring that he was not unnecessarily removed from the regular educational environment. District witnesses demonstrated to the court that they carefully considered S.M.'s needs when crafting an IEP that permitted him to have meaningful benefit in his education in the least restrictive environment, as required by the IDEA.

CASE EXAMPLE

S.C. v. Oxford Area School District

S.C. was evaluated and diagnosed with reading and writing learning disabilities just before starting third grade. His next reevaluation was at the end of fifth grade, where it was found that he was making acceptable progress but still had learning disabilities. At the end of eighth grade, S.C. was evaluated again, and was found to have learning disabilities in reading comprehension, written language, and math problem solving.[14]

S.C. was ordinarily happy, social, and respectful at school, but his teachers were now noticing problems in the classroom, such as he was often tired, unfocused, inattentive, and easily distracted. The district, working with S.C.'s mother, crafted an IEP for ninth grade with goals in reading comprehension, writing, math computation, and math application. To address his

---

14 While reevaluations should be performed at least once every three years, I should point out that this is not always the timeline kept, and that schools are usually out of compliance on this issue.

lack of focus, his teachers would clarify and repeat directions, seat him near the front of classrooms, and prompt him orally to keep him focused. However, S.C. missed well over one hundred class periods in ninth grade (the transcript doesn't detail why, but intimates anxiety issues). He struggled with algebra, so a special education teacher worked one-on-one with him in math, but he failed algebra and four other classes. His grade point average (GPA) was 0.97. Nonetheless, he made progress toward his program goals and advanced to tenth grade by taking summer classes. S.C. continued making progress, and his absences decreased and his grades increased, giving him a GPA of 2.04. He made more progress in eleventh grade, but S.C.'s absences increased, including in twenty-nine academic-support classes. The school provided additional resources and supplementary aids, which helped S.C. continue to make progress on his program goals. He improved his nonfiction writing, achieved some math goals, and reached his reading goal. His GPA was 2.19.

Nonetheless, S.C.'s mother filed a due process complaint in December of S.C.'s twelfth grade claiming the programs were inadequate and failed to ensure that her son received a FAPE. The hearing officer denied all relief, so S.C.'s mother pursued further remedy.

The issue before for the federal district court: Had the district taken steps that were reasonably calculated to enable S.C. to make meaningful academic progress, even if he did not progress as quickly as his peers? The district court ruling was again in the school district's favor, finding that while it was unfortunate S.C. did not progress as far or as fast as his mother hoped, the district met its legal obligation. The court noted that under the IDEA, school districts must provide an educational program reasonably calculated to enable a child to make progress appropriate to the child's circumstances. The court pointed out that reasonable does not mean perfect; a program need not and cannot guarantee a student's academic progress. S.C.'s slower progress did not prove that his programs were deficient; they were appropriate because they properly addressed his behavior and enabled him to progress academically. S.C. kept pace with his peers, went from failing several of his classes to passing all of them, and increased his GPA each year. S.C. achieved this success despite missing hundreds of classes, including his academic-support classes. Additionally, the programs addressed his behavioral issues, with teachers giving S.C. oral prompts, seating him near the front of the classroom, giving extra time for his assignments, and offering academic-support classes to help him stay organized and focused. There was no reason to think that these measures were inadequate or that S.C. missed classes because of his anxiety.

Note: Whether the standard of meaningful benefit has been met requires a court to make an objective analysis of the overall achievements or lack thereof. However, there is also subjective analysis on whether the administrative hearing officer or district court judge believes that a student has made meaningful progress toward educational goals.

Conclusions

After reading Steps One through Four, it's easy to see how parents can become overwhelmed in trying to get their children's educational needs met. When making a challenge about the denial of a FAPE, my overall suggestion for parents is to make careful notes using the Thought Questions throughout this book. Reread the court cases, especially the ones that are closest to your situation. Check the analysis used in the *Endrew F.* case. For example, is your child's IEP sufficient for educational meaningful benefit, and is it being implemented appropriately? The overall significance of the *Endrew F.* case is that standards have changed requiring courts to raise the standard for school districts from an IEP needing to achieve a goal of *de minimus* benefit to meaningful benefit. The question to always keep in mind: Is your child receiving meaningful benefit in his or her educational goals?

Glossary of Terms

ADA: Americans with Disabilities Act

ADHD: Attention-Deficit/Hyperactivity Disorder

BCBA: Board Certified Behavior Analyst

CBI: Community-Based Inclusion

CSE: Committee on Special Education

ER: Evaluation Report

FAPE: Free Appropriate Public Education

FBA: Functional Behavior Assessment

IDEA: Individuals with Disabilities Education Act

IEP: Individualized Education Program

IEE: Independent Educational Evaluation

IHO: Impartial Hearing Officer

NOREP/PWN: Notice of Recommended Educational Placement/Prior Written Notice

SDI: Specially Designed Instruction

SRO: State Review Officer

Case Citations

Step One: What is Child Find?

Montuori v. District of Columbia, 2018 U.S.Dist. LEXIS 165034 (D.C. Cir. 2018); pg. 9

Durbrow v. Cobb County School District, 887 F.3d 1182 (11 Cir. 2018); pg. 11

Step Two: Why is an Evaluation Important?

Y.N. v. Board of Education of the Harrison Central School District, 2018 U.S.Dist. LEXIS 164453 (S.D.N.Y. 2018); pg. 28

B.G. v. Board of Education of the City of Chicago, 901 F.3d 903 (7th Cir. 2018); pg. 25

N.D.S. v. Academy for Science and Agriculture Charter School, 2018 U.S.Dist. LEXIS 200987 (D.Minn. 2018); pg. 20

Luo v. Owen J. Roberts School District, 737 Fed.Appx. 111 (3rd Cir. 2018); pg. 30

M.B. v. City School District of New Rochelle, 2018 U.S.Dist. LEXIS 53564 (S.D.N.Y. 2018); pg. 31

Colonial School District v. G.K., 2018 U.S.Dist. LEXIS 72754 (E.D.Pa. 2018); pg. 18

Step Three: What is an IEP v. a 504 Service Agreement?

Pottsgrove School District v. D.H., 2018 U.S.Dist. LEXIS 154991 (E.D.Pa. 2018); pg. 45

E.I.H. v. Fair Lawn Board of Education, 747 Fed.Appx. 68 (3rd Cir. 2018); pg. 42

Smith v. District of Columbia, 2018 U.S.Dist. LEXIS 168005 (D.C. 2018); pg. 41

Carr v. New Glarus School District, 2018 U.S.Dist. LEXIS 175818 (W.D.Wisc. 2018); pg. 38

Brown v. Elk Grove Unified School District, 2018 U.S.Dist. LEXIS 27090 (E.D.Ca. 2018); pg. 53

Doe v. United States Secretary of Transportation, 2018 U.S.Dist. LEXIS 206239 (S.D.N.Y. 2018); pg. 55

Pollack v. Regional School Unit 75, 886 F.3d 75 (1st Cir. 2018); pg. 48

Crochran v. Columbus City Schools, 748 Fed.Appx. 682 (6th Cir. 2018); pg. 61

Cameron D. v. Arab City Board of Education, 2018 U.S.Dist. LEXIS 164827 (N.D.Ala. 2018); pg. 62

H.P. v. Naperville Community Unit School District #203, 910 F.3d 957 (7th Cir. 2018); pg. 52

Step Four: How Do You File a Complaint?

L.H. v. Hamilton County Department of Education, 2018 U.S.Dist. LEXIS 197705 (E.D.TN. 2018); pg. 71

Rena C. v. Colonial School District, 890 F.3d 404 (3rd Cir. 2018); pg. 67

Lincoln-Sudbury Regional School District v. W., 2018 U.S.Dist. LEXIS 72828 (D.Mass. 2018); pg. 70

Matthews v. Douglas County School District RE 1, 2018 U.S.Dist. LEXIS 171787 (D.Colo. 2018); pg. 80

Exhaustion and the Importance of Doing Things in the Right Order

S.D. v. Haddon Heights Board of Education, 722 Fed.Appx. 119 (3rd Ci. 2018); pg. 79

Doucette v. Jacobs, 288 F.Supp.3d 459 (D.Mass. 2018); pg. 75

Swanger v. Warrior Run School District, 2018 U.S.Dist. LEXIS 170277 (M.D.Pa. 2018); pg. 56

Bullying and Your Disabled Child

Spring v. Allegany-Limestone Central School District,
   2017 U.S.Dist. LEXIS 209250 (W.D.N.Y. 2017); pg. 86
Bowe v. Eau Claire Area School District,
   2018 U.S.Dist. LEXIS 19671 (W.D.Wisc. 2018); pg. 85
T.C. v. Hempfield Area School District,
   2018 U.S.Dist. LEXIS 130817 (W.D.Pa. 2018); pg. 83

Post the Endrew F. Case and How Courts Have Considered Meaningful Benefit

S.C. v. Oxford Area School District, 751 Fed.Appx. 220 (3rd Cir. 2018); pg. 96
S.M. v. Arlotto, 2018 U.S.Dist. LEXIS 156827 (D.Md. 2018); pg. 94
F.L. v. Board of Education of the Great Neck Union Free School District, 735 Fed.Appx. 38 (2nd Cir. 2018); pg. 92
Somberg v. Utica Community Schools, 908 F.3d 162 (6th Cir. 2018); pg. 72.

U.S. Federal Circuits

Some of the cases were appealed to an appellate court in the federal circuit. The citation may read 1st Cir., 2nd Cir., 3rd Cir., etc. "Cir" stands for circuit and the numbers correspond to one of 12 circuits in which every state belongs. Federal cases start in the federal district court but can then get appealed to an appellate court within their circuit. Below is a list of all the circuits and the states within each circuit.

DISTRICT OF COLUMBIA CIRCUIT
Washington D.C.

1ST CIRCUIT
Maine, Massachusetts, New Hampshire, Puerto Rico, Rhode Island

2ND CIRCUIT
Connecticut, New York, Vermont

3RD CIRCUIT
Delaware, New Jersey, Pennsylvania, U.S. Virgin Islands

4TH CIRCUIT
Maryland, North Carolina, South Carolina, Virginia, West Virginia,

5TH CIRCUIT
Louisiana, Mississippi, Texas

6TH CIRCUIT
Kentucky, Michigan, Ohio, Tennessee

7TH CIRCUIT
Illinois, Indiana, Wisconsin

8TH CIRCUIT
Arkansas, Iowa, Minnesota, Missouri, Nebraska, North Dakota, South Dakota

9th Circuit
Alaska, Arizona, California, Guam, Hawaii, Idaho, Montana, Nevada, Oregon, Washington

10th Circuit
Colorado, Kansas, New Mexico, Oklahoma, Utah, Wyoming

11th Circuit
Alabama, Florida, Georgia

Acknowledgments

The idea for this book came from the countless parents I spoke to who had three main grieving points: (1) I don't understand what the cases mean; (2) I don't understand how to use the cases; (3) I feel outnumbered by the school district and their "team."

I understand. The IEP and 504 process from Child Find to Evaluation can be overwhelming to understand and, sometimes, accept. Then, comes the Compliance aspect, which can feel like a full-time job. I also understand and have a true respect for the notion that a parent should not feel like they need to get a lawyer involved in order for the school district to comply with their child's IEP or 504 Service Agreement. Free Appropriate Public Education is not always free.

I'm an attorney (and a mom) so I get it. When I was a prosecutor, I saw the costs in the juvenile courtroom of parents lamenting about the school not allowing their child to transition back to their traditional school or the school calling them everyday to "come get him." As a special education attorney, I presented at parent meetings with legal case law updates and the end questions always boiled down to, how can I use this information going forward?

Insert, this booklet. I wrote this to achieve two main goals:

Empower parents, intellectually, by providing the same legal information the school districts' lawyers know and, therefore, train the school district administration to know;

Empower parents, in application, at IEP meetings by providing relevant, useful questions they can ask themselves as they ponder whether "now" is the time to call an attorney

I would like to thank my editor, Lila Stromer, for her tremendous patience , support, and guidance in making sure I make legal language more easily comprehensible and digestible. She was the "delivery nurse" for this "baby" to whom I have tremendous gratitude.

I would also like to thank my husband, Kurt, for his support in believing in me and this book; and my parents and sister for supporting me throughout this process.

To all the parents of special needs children, I heard you. This book is for you.

About the Author

Jennifer Oneal Price is a special education attorney and principal attorney of the Law Office of Jennifer O. Price in the Pittsburgh metro area. As a former prosecutor, Attorney Price is an experienced trial lawyer who represents children with disabilities. Attorney Price's advocacy includes attending IEP meetings, disciplinary hearings, and vigorously defending clients in juvenile court. She also represents clients in civil rights matters, relating to violations of Title II of the ADA, Section 504 of the Rehabilitation Act of 1973, and constitutional violations.

Attorney Price began her legal career as an Assistant District Attorney for Allegheny County in Pittsburgh, Pennsylvania. As a prosecutor, she was the sole trial counsel in both jury and bench trials. She prosecuted hundreds of cases, including major felonies, such as attempted homicides, robberies, drug and gun violations, and sexual abuse against children.

Attorney Price is very familiar with the courts and believes in making sure every child has an opportunity to succeed both in school and in life. Her boutique law firm provides services protecting and defending against abuses of the criminal justice system, as well as the educational system. With 10 years of experience, Attorney Price's advocacy has resulted in successes, including getting criminal charges withdrawn, preventing children from getting expelled out of school and federal lawsuits or due process hearings, resulting in successful settlements. She is an award recipient of Who's Next: Law by The Incline and Fab 40 from the New Pittsburgh Courier. She is a frequent legal commentator on Rush to Judgment and NightTalk, produced by PCNC, a Pittsburgh NBC affiliate. She is also the author of "The Vicious Cycle Inside Allegheny County Juvenile Court for Black Girls and their Mothers. I Saw it Up Close," an in-depth reporting article of Attorney Price's experience as both a prosecutor and mother.

She is an active member of her community, where she has served on the boards of Literacy Council and Pittsburgh Mercy Health. She has also been a hearing committee member of the Disciplinary Board of the Supreme Court of Pennsylvania. She is a member of Mothers of Preschoolers (Murrysville chapter), American Association of University Women (Murrysville chapter) and board member of the Murrysville Community Library Foundation Board.

www.ingramcontent.com/pod-product-compliance
Lightning Source LLC
Chambersburg PA
CBHW052101070526
44584CB00017B/2285